LAFAYETTE

in America

NORTH STAR BOOKS

LAFAYETTE
in America

ANDRÉ MAUROIS

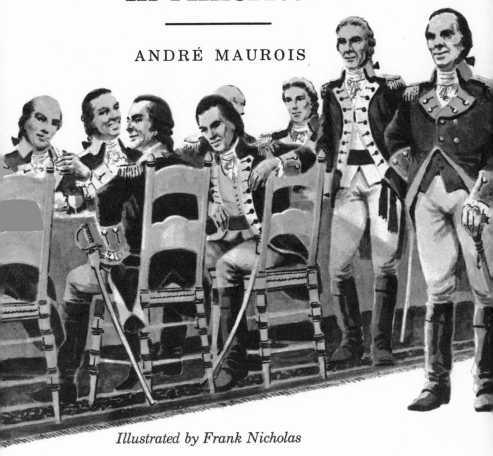

Illustrated by Frank Nicholas

1 9 6 0

Houghton Mifflin Company Boston

The Riverside Press Cambridge

41, 316

Books by

ANDRÉ MAUROIS

Silences du Colonel Bramble

Ariel, or the Life of Shelley

The Life of Disraeli

Dickens

A History of England

Chateaubriand

History of the United States

A History of France

The Quest for Proust

Lelia, or the Life of George Sand

Olympio, or the Life of Victor Hugo

Alexander Dumas

Contents

———

When khaki-clad American troops came to the rescue of France in 1917, their Commander, General John J. Pershing, said quietly:

"Lafayette, we are here!"

One hundred and forty years had intervened since Lafayette had crossed the Atlantic to aid Washington and his ragged little army in their unequal struggle against the British. But America had never forgotten that assistance, and here was an excellent opportunity to repay Lafayette and his country for the help they gave us during the American Revolution.

It would be difficult to find a more qualified author than André Maurois for a book on Lafayette. He knows our language, our literature and our political ideals. And he has always been a bridge between his own beloved France and the English-speaking world. Like Lafayette himself, he has helped to forge stronger links between sister republics.

A new book by André Maurois is always a literary event. We are proud to welcome him to our distinguished list of North Star historians.

STERLING NORTH
General Editor

LAFAYETTE
in America

1
Two Children and a Marriage

IN 1765 there lived in the Castle of Chavaniac, in the French province of Auvergne, an eight-year-old boy with reddish hair. He bore a great name and a proud title, for he was "the high and powerful lord, Gilbert du Motier, Marquis de Lafayette." His father, an officer in the king's army, had been killed in 1759 (two years after the birth of his son) at the Battle of Minden, fighting against the English. That is how Gilbert, even though he was so young, had already assumed the title of Marquis and had become the Lord of the Manor of Chavaniac.

The castle, a huge, imposing pile, dominated the dark, gloomy countryside. High mountains surrounded it. All winter long, they were covered with snow. Gilbert lived in the castle with his grandmother, two old aunts, and the Abbé Fayon, his tutor. The family, although noble, was poor. Of course, Gilbert's mother was rich, but she lived in Paris with her father, the Marquis de La Rivière, who was a stingy old man, and she came to Chavaniac only for a month or so every summer.

With three elderly ladies and a tutor, life was hardly gay for Gilbert, but he didn't complain.

His mind was filled with dreams of the glorious career he was going to have in the king's army. He never forgot that he was the son of a gallant soldier; and he never forgot, either, that he had to live up to his great name and assume the responsibilities it implied.

When he traveled around the countryside near Chavaniac, dressed in a silk suit, a three-cornered hat, silver-buckled shoes, and knee breeches, all the peasants recognized him and greeted him as their master. His tutor, the Abbé Fayon, used to tell him stories from Roman history, and Gilbert loved these accounts of the great deeds of the past.

When he came back from his walks that snowy winter of 1765, the old ladies would ask him, "Are they still talking about the Beast?" For during that winter, an enormous animal roved through the mountains of Auvergne, raiding the farms, carrying off chickens and even pigs. There had always been wolves in this wild country, but this beast appeared more terrible than anything the peasants had ever seen. Some said that it was a hyena that had escaped from a traveling zoo, but the peasants insisted that the monster was of some unknown species. When they heard the animal howling in the nearby forests, they trembled with fear.

"Take good care," his grandmother used to say to the Abbé, "not to meet the Beast when you go walking with Gilbert."

"But Grandmother, I *want* to meet him," replied Gilbert, "because I want to kill him."

It was hard to stop the boy from going out alone with his little sword at his side to roam over the snow-covered roads to track down the Beast and kill him.

"I am the lord of this village," he would say, "and it is my duty to defend it."

All winter long he continued to hope that he might meet the Beast on one of his walks. Then one day a hunter shot the animal. It was indeed a wolf of an extraordinary size, and they sent its skin to Paris to be shown to the King and the Queen.

The young nobleman lived for three more years

with the old ladies, all dressed in black, in the gloomy castle in Auvergne. Then, when he was eleven, his mother decided to send him away to school, to the Collège du Plessis in Paris. That didn't please Gilbert at all. At Chavaniac everyone knew him and spoke to him when he passed by. In Paris he would be a stranger. Living alone in the country had made him aloof and shy. But at school he worked hard. He never had to be punished—"and that is just as well," he said, "for I never could have stood it."

One day he had to write a composition on the subject: "Describe a perfect horse." He wrote that the perfect horse would throw its rider if he tried to use the whip. He had a high regard for independence. When one of his classmates was unjustly punished, he organized a protest meeting among the pupils of the school. He read Jean Jacques Rousseau and Voltaire, and even though he was of noble birth, he loved their democratic ideals.

Naturally, when it came time to choose a career, he went into the army. His grandfather,

the Marquis de La Rivière, sent him to an officer in the musketeers for his military education. On the days when military reviews were held, Gilbert was excused from school in order to march with his regiment. He wore a handsome scarlet uniform covered with gold braid. He was a fine tall boy, of proven courage, but, his friends thought, a little awkward and self-conscious and much more serious than you would expect anyone of his age to be.

In 1770, when he was not yet thirteen years old, his mother died. A few weeks later, the Marquis de La Rivière died too, leaving Gilbert an immense fortune. Within a few days, the poor young nobleman from Auvergne had become one of the richest peers of France. What a change!

In order to complete his military training, he was sent to spend a year in the Military Academy at Versailles. There he met the sons of the most illustrious families of the kingdom. In the riding school, he met the Comte d'Artois, the grandson of Louis XV. Lafayette did not ride as well as his brilliant companion, but since he had an income of 120,000 pounds — which was a great deal of money — he was able to buy handsome horses, which he lent to all his friends. As a result, even though he was shy and not a very good mixer, he was very popular at the military academy.

When he was fourteen and a half, his uncle, the Comte de La Rivière, decided that the time had come to find him a wife. That may strike us as incredible, but in Lafayette's time, and in the aristocratic world to which he belonged, marriage was not a question of love or of personal preference, but rather of rank, family alliances, and of the financial advantages involved in merging two fortunes. After the ceremony, if the couple were too young, they continued to live with their parents as before, but both families were satisfied that "everything was settled" as far as the children's social position and financial situation were concerned.

Lafayette, because of his fortune and his great name, was already a "wonderful catch." His uncle soon reached an understanding with the Duc d'Ayen, the oldest son of the Maréchal de Noailles (who was very powerful at Court), to arrange a marriage between Gilbert and the Duc's daughter, Adrienne d'Ayen, who was then only twelve. However, Adrienne's mother, the Duchesse d'Ayen, a fine woman, deeply religious and highly intelligent, was opposed to it. Contrary to the customs of the time, she had brought up her daughters herself and had given them an excellent education. She was shocked that her husband intended to marry Adrienne off so young.

"Not only is she still a child herself," objected the Duchesse, "but this young Marquis de Lafayette has always lived a very sheltered life; he has never received the proper training, and this vast fortune which has come into his hands may be the cause of his undoing unless some responsible person can exercise control over him. I know that people say he has an excellent character. But still it's too soon, they are too young, and I refuse to consent to their marriage."

This threw the Duc d'Ayen into a violent rage. He was a man who was seldom at home with his family; he preferred living in Versailles at the Court. He vowed that he would not set foot in his own home again until his wife changed her mind. This state of affairs lasted for a year. Finally, a compromise was worked out. The marriage was decided upon, but it would not take place until the young Marquis had finished his studies. Meanwhile, Adrienne would remain with her mother.

So Gilbert was taken one day to call at the

Noailles mansion, a lovely house which still stands on the aristocratic old rue St.-Honoré in Paris. There he met his future wife. In the fashion of the time, he respectfully kissed her hand. He noticed that she was dainty and delicate, and that she had lovely eyes. The Duchesse d'Ayen immediately liked this young man who seemed so different from the others. When she agreed to the marriage, matters were smoothed out between herself and her husband. As for Adrienne, she was immediately attracted to the young officer, and their marriage was finally celebrated on April 11, 1774. The bride was then fourteen and a half and the groom was not yet seventeen!

That summer, Gilbert de Lafayette, who had been named captain in the Noailles regiment, made several trips to Metz, in Lorraine, where his men were on garrison duty. The following winter, this very young couple was presented at Court where, thanks to the influence of the Duc d'Ayen, they were regularly invited to the balls given weekly by Queen Marie Antoinette.

In this brilliant and frivolous society, the

Marquis de Lafayette felt out of place and ill at ease. He talked very little, for he thought that the conversation carried on around him was silly and empty. He knew he did not have the elegance and polish necessary to impress the Queen and the smart set that gathered around the Comte d'Artois. One of his friends, the Comte de Ségur, said that "Lafayette seemed cold and shy, but underneath the mask, there lay hidden strong character and a fiery spirit."

It was true, but the Court could not see it. Queen Marie Antoinette and her brothers-in-law (the Comte d'Artois and the Comte de Provence) had completely transformed life at Versailles. They put on ballets for the amusement of the Queen. Lafayette was not a graceful dancer, so Marie Antoinette did not care for him. His clumsiness made her laugh. His brother-in-law, the elegant Vicomte de Noailles, had all the success. He danced well, he drank well, and Lafayette was a little jealous of him. In order not to be completely overshadowed by the Vicomte, he used to force himself to drink and then would tell everyone, "Be sure to let Noailles know how well I can hold my liquor!"

The fact is that Lafayette was not meant for this frivolous Court life. He liked practical, serious things, and he well realized that he was out of place at Versailles. When he received a flattering invitation to become a member of the household of the Comte de Provence, the brother of the King, he deliberately made a remark designed to antagonize the very prince who wanted to do him a favor. The Maréchal de Noailles was very irritated by this attitude, but Adrienne supported her husband. She liked Court life no better than he. She adored Lafayette and it saddened her when he was called back to his regiment in Metz during the summer of 1775.

2

Why Not?

ON THE FOURTH of July, 1776, when the Declaration of Independence was proclaimed in Philadelphia, young Captain Lafayette was in Metz with his regiment. He was only nineteen, but because of his family connections and his intelligence and enthusiasm, the military governor of the city, the Comte de Broglie, treated him like a son. Moreover, Lafayette was very much at home at Metz because two of his best friends (who were also relatives), the Comte de Ségur and the Vicomte de Noailles, belonged to the same regiment.

One day the Duke of Gloucester, who was the brother of the King of England, passed through

Metz. The Comte de Broglie gave a dinner party in his honor, and since he liked to have young people around him, he invited Lafayette, Ségur, and Noailles. The Duke, who had just received mail from London, began to talk freely of what was happening in the American colonies. This English lord, who was sympathetic to the American point of view, thought that the policies of his brother, King George III, were absurd, and did not hesitate to reveal his feelings to the French officers.

They were enthusiastic about what he said. Lafayette was particularly interested and continued to ask questions. "So the people of Boston have obtained arms? They're fighting bravely? Does the Declaration of Independence speak of liberty? Does it say that all men are created equal?" But this was wonderful! Ever since boyhood, Lafayette had been reading Plutarch and Rousseau concerning the rights of man. Besides, he had never liked the English because his father had been killed fighting against them, and because they had taken Canada away from France. So he decided that very evening to offer his help to the Americans who were fighting to obtain their independence from Great Britain.

The next day he talked over his plans with the Comte de Broglie, his commanding officer. "Never again shall I have such a wonderful chance to win fame and honor while I am still young. Besides, the destiny of France is at stake over there. If the American colonists are defeated, it will be disastrous for our navy and for our possessions in the Caribbean."

The Comte de Broglie could scarcely have agreed more thoroughly with Lafayette. He would have liked to set out for America himself, but he remembered that he had some of the responsibilities of a father to this young officer who had no parents to advise him.

"My boy," he said, "I saw your father killed at Minden, and I cannot give my approval to your plan. It might mean the end of the sole remaining branch of your family. Besides, don't forget that you have a young wife who is expecting a baby. You can't go off and leave her alone."

"But my wife has her mother. And besides, both of them are too idealistic not to approve of what I plan to do," replied Lafayette.

When he returned to Paris, he found the whole city just as enthusiastic about the American Revolution as he was. They even changed the name of the popular game of whist to "Boston." Everywhere the young noblemen talked of "democracy," "independence," "revolution." They compared the American Congress to the Roman Senate. French volunteers crowded the Paris office of Silas Deane, the American representative in France, who, unfortunately, did not know a single word of French. Deane handed out officers' commissions to almost anyone who asked.

The French government, on the other hand, was extremely cautious. They were delighted, of course, to see the English in difficulties, and they secretly encouraged the American rebels. But they did not want a shooting war with England. King Louis XVI believed that a ruling monarch could not openly lend his support to the rebellious subjects of another king. Nevertheless, the French government had agreed to furnish the revolutionists with uniforms, cannon, and gunpowder through the operations of a fake business firm, Rodrigue Hortalès and Company. Of course, the Hortalès company did not exist; the aid came from the French government. But when the English protested, the French replied very seriously that they knew nothing about it, that this dangerous Hortalès was probably Spanish, and that in any event they had no idea who he was.

Lafayette, when he became aware of the

enthusiasm of the French public for the American cause and learned of the support the government was secretly giving it, believed he could easily volunteer. The Comte de Broglie, having tried to keep him from going, now saw that the young Captain had definitely made up his mind and decided that he might as well try to help him. He knew a German, a fine soldier, who called himself Baron de Kalb. As a matter of fact, he was not a baron and his name was simply Kalb, but he spoke English well and was in close touch with the Americans. He agreed to present Lafayette, Noailles, and Ségur to the American commissioners.

So De Kalb introduced Lafayette to Silas Deane. Deane was struck by the sincerity and the idealism of this young man who said with such modesty, "I can offer you nothing but my enthusiasm. I have no experience, but perhaps my presence can be of use to you in America, and my example helpful to you here in France." The son-in-law of the Duc d'Ayen! The grandson of the Maréchal de Noailles! Silas Deane had never had a volunteer of such high quality. He was literally dazzled and offered a commission of major general to this nineteen-year-old officer.

Naturally, Lafayette was wildly happy. Soon, he told himself, adventure, fame, and glory would be his. Nothing seemed impossible, for he was afraid of nothing. He took the Latin phrase *Cur non* ("Why not?") as his motto. Ségur and Noailles, however, were pulled up short because of the opposition of their families. Since they had no personal income, they had to obey their parents. But Lafayette had no family to oppose him, and his yearly income of 120,000 pounds made it possible for him to do anything he liked — even purchase a ship if necessary. If he had to, he would leave alone.

Nevertheless, he still had to overcome strong opposition on the part of his wife's family. The Duc d'Ayen was furious, and so was the Maréchal de Noailles. Only the Duchesse d'Ayen and Adrienne gave their approval, although Adrienne was filled with sadness to think that her husband was going so far away, particularly so soon after the birth of their little girl, whom they had named Henriette. Adrienne was still weak and far from well, but her courage never faltered. The Duc d'Ayen, who was very powerful at Court, succeeded in having the French government issue an order forbidding Lafayette to leave the country.

Lafayette refused to take this order seriously. He thought that the government was naturally obliged to disapprove publicly of what he was doing, in order not to provoke an incident with the English. But he thought that basically all of France approved. However, the French navy would not make a ship available to him. So, after consulting with the Comte de Broglie, he sent an officer to Bordeaux to buy a vessel in which De Kalb, Lafayette himself, and their staff might sail for America to volunteer in the Army of Independence.

The purchase of the ship and of necessary supplies would take at least a month, so Lafayette decided to go to London to visit his wife's uncle, the Marquis de Noailles, who was then the French Ambassador to the Court of Saint James.

He thought it would be excellent strategy to take a trip to England at the very time he was engaged in fitting out his expedition against the British. Besides, he was perfectly frank with his London friends and let it be known everywhere that he was a supporter of the Americans. When they won the Battle of Trenton, Lafayette was openly jubilant.

Nor was he the only one. Even in England the liberals understood that the suppression of liberty in America endangered liberty in the mother country as well. The leading Whig families extended their hospitality to this young nobleman who dared to say what he thought. And even the Tories admired the coolness of this French officer who dared beard the British lion in his den at a time when there was much talk of war between France and England. His uncle, the Ambassador, presented him to King George III. Lafayette thought that the monarch was pleasant enough but rather tiresome. He was, in fact, a harmless old fellow who was a little out of his mind.

From London, Lafayette wrote to the Duc d'Ayen: "You will be astonished, my dear father, at what I have to tell you . . . I have been named a major general in the Army of the United States of America . . . For the time being, dear father, I am in London, still waiting for my friends. As soon as I hear from them, I shall leave here and, without stopping at Paris, proceed directly to embark on the vessel which I have bought and which is now being fitted out." He added that he was very sad to leave his family whom he loved "more tenderly than anyone could ever imagine. But this voyage will not be too long—people often set out on pleasure trips that are longer than this . . . Farewell, dear father, your affection is precious to me and I hope that I shall always enjoy it."

In spite of these tender words, the Duc d'Ayen was extremely irritated and decided to do everything he could to prevent Lafayette from leaving. Moreover, the young man had returned to Paris (despite what he had written his father-in-law to the contrary) and was staying incognito with

De Kalb, who planned to leave with him.

One morning around seven o'clock, Lafayette suddenly burst into the room of his friend Ségur. He shut the door and sat down beside the bed.

"I'm going to America," he said. "No one knows about it. But you're one of my best friends, and I couldn't leave without telling you my secret."

"And how are you going to arrange it?"

Lafayette, who had complete confidence in his friend, explained his plan in detail, and then left to tell another intimate friend, the Vicomte de Noailles. He dared not see his wife because of the attitude of his father-in-law, but he had written her a long letter from London. She was expecting a second child, and it was hard for her to accept her husband's decision to leave. But her courageous mother comforted her and assured her that Lafayette's departure was not at all the foolish whim of an impulsive young man, but rather a well-thought-out action that was proof of his courage and idealism.

Lafayette had scarcely left for Bordeaux with

De Kalb when the Duc d'Ayen hurried to ask the King's minister, Maurepas, to put a stop to his son-in-law's plans. From London, the Ambassador was writing outraged letters. It was inconceivable, he thundered! He had received this young man under his own roof and had even arranged for him to be presented to His Majesty the King of England, and now he was setting off to fight on the side of a band of rebels against legally constituted British authority. It put him, as ambassador, in a very difficult position. He made his displeasure known to the family of Lafayette as well as to the Court. The military authorities at Bordeaux were alerted and instructed to stop the young rebel and even to arrest him if necessary.

Lafayette had just time to get out of Bordeaux and sail to the little Spanish port of Los Passajes. De Kalb took charge of having stores put on board. But the young Marquis was depressed. He had embarked on a heroic action which he believed would serve his country. And now the government of that country wanted to arrest him for it. His proud nature could not accept this. He took the risk of returning to Bordeaux to get in touch with his father-in-law and to convince the Minister. De Kalb grumbled at the idea.

"You'll never come back," he said.

But at Bordeaux, Lafayette found a messenger from his old friend, the Comte de Broglie. It was the Vicomte de Mauroy, an officer who, like Lafayette, had also volunteered to join the Americans.

"Everything will be all right," said Mauroy. "The Comte de Broglie has seen the Minister. Your father-in-law is the only one responsible for all this trouble. The Minister himself wouldn't have said anything. As a matter of fact, everybody in Paris and at the Court approves of what you are doing. You can leave with a clear conscience."

This time, Lafayette was reassured. He set off with Mauroy by mail coach for the Spanish frontier. At Saint Jean de Luz, the last town before the border, they stopped to change horses. While they were at the inn, a cavalry detachment rode up to inquire from the innkeeper's daughter if she had seen a young officer of noble birth, very tall, with reddish hair. But on his arrival, Lafayette had looked at the girl and put his finger to his lips. She had understood that some romantic adventure was going on, and replied, "No, I haven't seen anyone."

The cavalrymen chatted a few minutes with her, then rode off. A moment later, Lafayette leaped into the saddle and galloped across the border. He was safe! Mauroy followed him in the mail coach.

De Kalb was astonished when they both strode down the waterfront of Los Passajes. He had given up hope of seeing them again. In two days their ship, the *Victory*, was loaded, and Lafayette gave the order to raise the anchor. It was the 20th of April, 1777.

3
Lafayette Discovers America

LAFAYETTE'S SHIP, the *Victory,* was commanded by Captain Le Boursier. Lafayette gave instructions to set his course for Charleston, South Carolina. The Captain, an old sea dog, realized that the Marquis was only a boy. He replied that the ship's papers indicated that they must sail by way of the Windward Islands and that the papers had to be respected.

"If I don't follow the course given on the papers," Captain Le Boursier insisted, "I am personally responsible. What would I do if a French man-of-war asked for my credentials?"

Lafayette was very well aware that he too would be arrested if the ship were forced to put

into a French port. The news of his flight had gone ahead of him, carried by frigates faster than the *Victory*. Speaking with courage and authority, he said that the ship belonged to him and that if the Captain did not obey his orders he would immediately put him in irons and replace him with his second in command.

This blunt command induced the Captain to think matters over. He confessed that the reason he was so anxious to go by way of the West Indies was because he had taken on board merchandise worth about $8000 which he planned to sell at a handsome profit. Mere financial considerations never bothered Lafayette.

"If that's all that's worrying you, I'll personally reimburse you for your loss of eight thousand dollars."

The Captain yielded, but not without making some new objections. If they set their course directly for the American coast, they ran the grave danger of being overtaken by a British man-of-war. The *Victory* was clumsy and slow and carried only two cannon. She could neither outrun an adversary nor defend herself against one. They decided that if attacked they would blow up the ship. A trusty-looking seaman from Holland was ordered to make ready several barrels of gunpowder for this purpose.

By now the *Victory* was in mid-ocean. Leaning over the rail, the young Marquis looked out over the vast expanse of water and thought of the destiny he had chosen for himself. What would he find on the other side of the ocean? Certainly there would be brave men in love with liberty. But did they really stand a chance of winning the war? The latest news was not good. The English were sending a well-trained professional army to crush a few thousand patriotic volunteers without arms, without uniforms, even without shoes for their feet. Everyone said that the American commander-in-chief, George Washington, was a hero. But what could the bravest hero do without weapons, without money, without a navy?

Lafayette was particularly concerned about reactions in France. What was the Court saying about him? Surely his departure had caused much talk. Some people would be critical, others were probably laughing at him. And he wondered about Adrienne, his wife. Did she understand why he hadn't seen her before he left? And even though he knew that he could not mail anything before they landed, Lafayette began to write her a long letter.

"I write you from so far away, my love, and even worse than the distance is the uncertainty of knowing when I shall have news from you . . . I keep asking myself so many questions. How did you take the news of my departure? Do you love me less because of it? Will you forgive me? . . . The waters of the ocean are melancholy and the sea and I are sad together."

In fact, the few soldiers on board the *Victory* were very sad indeed. During the first days out, all these heroes were seasick. They ran into head winds which slowed the vessel. After forty days at sea, they were still at least ten days from their destination, Charleston.

Suddenly one morning the watch sighted a

small ship on the horizon. Everyone prepared for battle. The Dutchman took his post beside the barrels of gunpowder, a fuse in his hand. The ship drew closer. Fortunately, it was American. Lafayette wanted to sail in company with it, but the *Victory* was too slow to keep pace.

It was the beginning of June. The sailors began to recognize certain signs that they were approaching land. Warm breezes surrounded them and birds flew near the ship. Lafayette wrote a final letter:

"June 7. I am still in the midst of this mournful plain. To cheer myself a little, I think of you and my friends. I think of the happiness of coming back to you. How marvelous it will be to arrive unexpectedly and rush home to take you in my arms! . . . I hope that for my sake you'll be 'a good American' . . . the happiness of America is bound up with the happiness of the entire human race. This country is destined to become the cherished home of liberty . . . Farewell, for now the darkness prevents me from going on, since I have forbidden any lights to be shown these last few nights. You see how cautious I am! Adieu, then. If my fingers obey the dictates of my heart, I need no light to write that I love you and will love you always."

Fifty days at sea! To fill the long hours, Lafayette had tried to learn English. To gain fluency, he practiced talking it with De Kalb. He learned the preamble to the Declaration of Independence by heart. Might his services not be needed at some future time to write such a declaration for his own country? Would it not be a fitting task for a hero who had learned this lesson through aiding the American struggle for independence? *Why not?*

What a fine land I am about to discover, he thought — a country where there is neither king nor court and where every man is equal!

At last, on Friday, June 13, at 2:30 in the afternoon, the *Victory* approached a flat, green coast, and dropped anchor in a small bay. It was not the port of Charleston where they had hoped to land, for there was no sign of any city. In that case where were they? The Marquis set out in a rowboat with De Kalb and two men to find the answer. As soon as he set foot on American soil, Lafayette cried out with deep feeling, "I swear that I shall conquer or perish in the name of independence!"

Old De Kalb, more cynical and more practical

as well, pointed out that the first thing to do was to discover where they were. He ordered the men to proceed up the silent, deserted river which flowed into the bay. It was hot, and the air was heavy and humid. Not until evening did they discover any sign of human life — four Negro fishermen! De Kalb had great difficulty making himself understood, but finally he found out that the Negroes were slaves of a planter living farther up the river. He asked to be taken to their master.

They continued rowing up the river in the oppressive heat until midnight. Finally they saw the lights of the plantation house. They leaped ashore. Dogs barked. In the darkness a voice cried out:

"Who's there? Where are you going?"

They answered, and the challenging voice in the darkness ordered them to come forward. In the shadows, they made out the form of a great house with a high-columned porch and a flight of steps mounting to it. In the front hall, Major Benjamin Huger was waiting for them. The name of his estate was Prospect Hill.

When the Marquis and De Kalb explained who
they were and the nature of their mission, the
Major gave them a friendly welcome and invited
them to be his guests. He told them that they
were in South Carolina, near the town of Georgetown, a little north of Charleston. While the
famished visitors were eating an excellent supper,
their host gave them the latest news of the war.
The English had had some success, one couldn't
deny it, but the Americans were strong and their
hopes were high.

"We have," said the Major, "a fine commander-in-chief, George Washington — a man full of energy and authority."

Lafayette felt better as he listened to the Major. Now things were happening the way he had dreamed they would: here, on his arrival, he was received by an American patriot; Washington actually was a great man; and Lafayette felt sure that he himself would later be welcomed by the supreme commander as a friend and ally.

A servant took him to his room, where, for the

first time in two months, he slept in a real bed,
between smooth linen sheets. The bed was hung
with mosquito netting. The Negro servants were
well trained. And when he woke in the morning
he saw from his window a charming landscape of
trees and flowers. Everything was going to be
fine.

Major Huger offered to lend them three horses
for the trip to Charleston. First, however, they
gave orders to the Captain of the *Victory*. On
Saturday morning Lafayette returned to his ship.
He told Le Boursier to sail for Charleston and to
keep a sharp watch for British cruisers. He and
De Kalb would travel on horseback. Any officers
who wanted to proceed to Charleston on foot
were given permission to do so.

Charleston was fifty miles to the south. The
Marquis and De Kalb arrived there in two days,
exhausted by the heat. The officers who had
walked looked like tramps when they finally
arrived. Their clothes were in rags and they were
covered with mosquito bites. They had thrown
away their boots because their feet were so

swollen that they could no longer wear them. People in the streets of Charleston hooted and whistled as the pitiful little band limped into town.

It must be said that the charming little city was then teeming with adventurers of every nationality. Many had come to offer their services to the Americans, not so much because they loved liberty, but rather to escape their own shady pasts and to make some easy money. At the time, the French had a bad reputation in Charleston and some of them, who had arrived before Lafayette, richly deserved it. But the idealism and the enthusiasm of the young Marquis quickly overcame all these prejudices. When the *Victory* dropped anchor in the port, and when the aristocratic Charleston families understood that a descendant of one of the noblest families of France had arrived in his own vessel to volunteer his services, they opened their houses and their hearts to him.

They gave him a magnificent banquet. He made a toast in English, and his French accent delighted everyone. In the streets of Charleston, people shouted *"Vive le Marquis"* when he passed. He was popular and it made him happy. He soon loved the little city, so fresh and clean, with its shady streets lined with graceful white houses. He liked the easy democracy of the day-to-day life. But he could not linger too long in Charleston. He had been named a major general in the American army. He had letters from Silas Deane and from Benjamin Franklin to present to the Continental Congress. He had to get to Philadelphia as soon as he could.

So — *"en route!"*

4
America Discovers Lafayette

CHARLESTON is more than 600 miles away from Philadelphia. Even by modern highways it is a long trip. But in eighteenth century America, where roads were scarcely more than tracks across dense forests, or fords across swamps, and where travelers lacked dependable maps and information, such a trip was both long and dangerous. Lafayette bought horses and carriages. He and De Kalb traveled in a big open barouche; two other coaches and a baggage wagon followed. Lafayette's servants rode on horseback beside him. A Negro horseman brought up the rear.

After a few days on the road, the carriages broke down completely. The party had to continue on horseback. Then the horses themselves collapsed from exhaustion and sickness. The Marquis purchased others, but these, too, soon gave out. They were forced to abandon their luggage and proceed on foot. Lafayette's companions, devoured by mosquitoes, ill with dysentery, swore that although they had endured many tough campaigns, they had never experienced anything like this. They kept their spirits high, however, and joked about the wonderful welcome that would be waiting for them in Philadelphia.

It took them thirty-two days to make the trip, and at last, on July 27, they arrived in Philadelphia, where the Continental Congress was in session. To their great surprise, no one in the streets paid the slightest attention to them. They tried to make themselves look presentable, and then went to Carpenters' Hall where Congress was meeting. As an introduction, they sent in the letters from Silas Deane, together with documents showing that they had been commissioned in the American army. After they had cooled their heels for some time in the street, a member of Con-

gress — a man the French called "the Sieur
Moose" — came out and told them they need not
bother to wait. They were to come back the
next morning.

They were on hand bright and early. Once
again they were kept waiting outside. The Marquis de Lafayette was unaccustomed to this sort
of treatment. Eventually "Moose" arrived, accompanied by another congressman named Lovell
who was supposed to speak French. He was presented as "the gentleman whose job it is to get
rid of people from your country." Without even
asking them to come in, Lovell began a little
speech in bad French.

"We know you. You're just a gang of impostors
and adventurers. We asked Silas Deane to send
us engineers. Instead, he sent us Du Coudray
who's not an engineer at all. Last year we did
need officers, but now we have plenty of them."

Whereupon he turned on his heel and went
inside, leaving Lafayette and his companions in
the street.

They were furious, and had every reason to be.

They had sacrificed their high positions in France
to fly to the aid of Liberty, and instead of being
welcomed, they were insulted. De Kalb tried to
calm them. He said he understood the nature of
the trouble. As a matter of fact, there *were* a large
number of international adventurers who had
flocked to Philadelphia as soldiers of fortune.
Du Coudray himself, even though an officer, was
of little worth. Silas Deane had accepted too
many volunteers without adequately checking
their qualifications. Philadelphia was swarming
with dissatisfied Europeans who stopped Lafa-

yette on the street to complain about the Americans. No wonder Congress was suspicious of newcomers. When Lafayette at last realized this, he declared, "I do not wish to be confused any longer with those who have come here to seek advantages for themselves rather than to offer their services."

Then he wrote an eloquent letter to the Speaker of Congress and asked him to read it aloud before the entire body. First explaining who he was, he then continued: "After all the sacrifices I have made in order to come to America, I have the right to ask two favors of the Congress. One is to serve at my own expense; the other is to serve as a volunteer."

Congress was agreeably surprised. The Europeans who had arrived before Lafayette had never shown such idealism and generosity. Several congressmen then read the letters of Silas Deane and Franklin — the Sieur Moose and Lovell had not even bothered to open them! — and they were stupefied to find that the young man they had received so rudely belonged to one of the noblest and most powerful families in France, a man who could be of inestimable assistance to the American cause. Congress, shamefaced at having treated such a good friend so badly, immediately voted the following resolution: "Whereas the Marquis de Lafayette, out of his great zeal because of his great devotion to the cause of liberty . . . has left his family and connections, and at his own expense come over to offer his services to the United States without pension or particular allowance, and is willing to risk his life in our cause—Resolved, that his services be accepted, and that in recognition of his zeal, and illustrious family and connections he have rank and commission of major general in the Army of the United States."

So his dream had come true!

At the same time, he learned that Washington himself had arrived in Philadelphia. An English fleet, with an army on board, had just appeared near the mouth of the Delaware River. Naturally the Commander-in-Chief wished to inspect his defenses.

The next day a banquet was given in Washington's honor and Lafayette was invited. At last he would meet his hero. He was not disappointed. He had never seen a reigning monarch who seemed more royal, more worthy of the responsibility of command. Washington was tall, with a handsome, noble countenance. He wore his uniform and his powdered wig with a distinction and a dignity that made the Marquis think of the Maréchal de Noailles. He spoke slowly and seriously; he seemed friendly and patient. Lafayette was conquered on the spot; in George Washington he had found a leader and, as he realized later, a second father.

He edged his way through the crowd in order to be introduced. Washington received him cordially, for the young man's youth and enthusiasm inspired confidence. After the long banquet, which closed with an endless series of toasts, Washington took Lafayette aside and told him that during the interval while they were arranging to find him a command, he would be a member of "the Commander-in-Chief's family"

—that is, of his own personal staff.

"I cannot promise you the luxury of Versailles or even the comfort to which you are accustomed. But I am sure that, as an American soldier, you will adapt yourself to your new situation and will accept gladly the rough manners and the hardships of a democratic army. Our officers share the life of their men. In our army, discipline is maintained, not by force, but by the spirit of equality which has united us. Since you have chosen to throw your lot in with ours, you will share our joys as well as our sorrows. Our victory will also be yours."

These words delighted Lafayette. Hardship, danger, fame—that was what he had come to the New World for! The General invited him to inspect the army. But what a sad sight! Eleven thousand men who scarcely knew how to stand at attention, some of them dressed in jackets of gray linsey-woolsey, some with no coats at all. How different from the smart Noailles regiment that Lafayette knew at Metz! But the men themselves seemed strong and determined.

Washington said very simply, "We're a little embarrassed not to make a better showing before an officer of the French Army."

Lafayette replied with tact and modesty, "I am here, sir, to learn rather than to teach."

He did everything in his power to encourage his friends to volunteer in the American army. Some followed his advice, but others were obliged to return to France. Lafayette, always anxious to do the honorable thing, offered to return with them, but De Kalb said, "No. After all the excitement of your departure from France, you must stay here and distinguish yourself."

So Lafayette wrote to Congress accepting his commission as a major general and asking for a command. In spite of all his sympathy for the young Frenchman, however, Washington was hesitant: "After all, he's scarcely twenty years old. I cannot entrust one of my divisions to such a young and inexperienced man."

On the following Sunday when the army, marching to the sound of drums and fifes, passed in review in Philadelphia, Washington invited Lafayette — very happy in his new uniform — to stand by his side. The crowds in the streets recognized the young Frenchman whose escape from

Paris and whose devotion to the American cause had made him very popular. They clapped their hands as he passed by, and the women whispered to each other, "That's the French Marquis." How Lafayette wished that his father-in-law could see him as he stood beside the Commander-in-Chief!

But the war news was bad. The English were advancing in force on Philadelphia. Washington, falling back a little, took a position on the heights overlooking the Brandywine River. The Marquis accompanied his commander on an inspection of his forward posts.

Washington was shortly informed by General Sullivan that the enemy had crossed the river and was turning the American line.

"Let me join General Sullivan," pleaded Lafayette. Washington gave his consent, and the young Frenchman galloped off toward the front lines. He found that Sullivan's men, realizing they were being outflanked, were fleeing in panic. It was the first time that Lafayette had been under fire, and he gave proof of remarkable courage. In his halting English, he rallied the men, crying out to them not to run away without putting up a fight. He managed to hold the rear guard long enough to permit the rest of the army to make an orderly retreat.

A fellow officer pointed to his leg which was covered with blood; in fact, Lafayette was wounded and had not realized it. He refused to

have himself cared for until the battle was over. When he was too weak to remain in the saddle, other officers forced him to leave. But in crossing a bridge that could be held, he insisted on pausing to rally the men and organize its defense.

At this moment, Washington arrived. He was much impressed by the courage of this youngster. He ordered Lafayette to the rear to have his wound cared for.

"Treat him as though he were my own son," he told the surgeons.

A few days later, Lafayette learned that the Commander-in-Chief had cited him in a dispatch addressed to the President of the Continental Congress. He considered himself well rewarded for the wound he had received.

He wrote to his wife: "The English honored me with a slight gunshot wound in the leg; it was nothing, my darling, since the bullet touched neither bone nor tendon. The only trouble is that I'll have to spend a few days in bed, which makes me furious. I hope, darling, that you won't worry about me."

5

The First Wound and the First Victory

TREAT HIM as though he were my own son," Washington had said. But it was not easy to find proper care even for the "son" of the Commander-in-Chief at a time when the English were advancing on Philadelphia and everyone was leaving town. Lafayette was taken by boat to Bristol, and from there to Bethlehem, Pennsylvania, a Moravian community. The Moravians were a small Protestant sect which had come to the New World to convert the Indians. They were men and women of real idealism and good will.

Lafayette was well taken care of. The wife of the owner of the biggest farm in Bethlehem invited him to her home and placed an entire floor at his disposal. The farmer's daughter, the charming Liesel Boeckel, was very kind to the young and interesting foreigner. From his bed, Lafayette avidly followed the military news. It was not very cheering. The English general, Cornwallis, had taken Philadelphia. Apparently the Americans would not be in a position to counterattack until winter arrived.

In Paris, a rumor was circulating that Lafayette was dead. Adrienne had just given birth to another daughter, Anastasie. Her mother wished to protect her from the bad news, particularly in the days following the birth of the child, so she took her daughter to the country. Lafayette at this time was also much concerned for fear that his wife and her family might feel he was fighting for a lost cause.

An officer friend on his way back to France carried to Adrienne detailed instructions as to what she should tell her friends about the situation in America.

First, he reassured her concerning his wound. "The doctors are astonished at how quickly it is healing. Every time they change the dressing, they exclaim about it. You'd think it was the most beautiful thing in the world . . . And now, since you are the wife of an American officer, I must give you a little lesson. People will tell you: 'The Americans have been defeated.' You should reply, 'That's true, but in a battle between two well-matched armies on a level terrain, experienced professional soldiers always have an initial advantage over volunteers. It's also true that the Americans have lost a large number of men, but still, their casualties are fewer than those of the enemy.' After that they'll probably say: 'That's all very well, but Philadelphia, the capital of America, the very bastion of liberty, has been captured.' And you should reply politely, 'Now you're talking nonsense. Philadelphia is a dreary town, completely unfortified. Its port has been closed long since. The only possible reason it is important is that the Congress met there. So you can see that this "bastion of liberty" isn't really vital to the American cause at all. Besides, they'll certainly recapture it shortly.' And if they still continue after that to fire questions at you, just show them to the door."

The Moravians, who were pacifists, did all they could to cure Lafayette of what they called his "warlike madness." They gave him soothing books to read about their missions in Greenland or their conversion of the Eskimos. But the hotheaded Marquis, although he respected his hosts very much, did not agree with them. Sitting with his wounded leg propped on a chair, surrounded with pious Moravian literature, Lafayette still

dreamed of military glory. He wanted France to get into the war. He wrote to the governor of the Windward Islands, a French possession in the Caribbean, proposing that he should undertake a little private expedition against the British West Indies, which could be conducted under the American flag to avoid international complications.

He even dared to write to the French minister, Maurepas, convinced that even though Maurepas had threatened him with arrest, he was really delighted that England was having "family troubles" with its American colonies. Lafayette considered himself to be filling the role of unofficial French ambassador to the United States. If anything embarrassing happened, of course, his government could take the position that they knew nothing of his activities. He was further convinced that he was serving the best interests of his country. Moreover, he was really justified in believing that he enjoyed Maurepas' admiration and sympathy.

"He'll end up auctioning off the furniture of

Versailles to help the American cause," observed the Minister with a smile, "for once he gets an idea in his head, you just can't argue with him."

Lafayette had many visitors at Bethlehem. An Irishman, Conway, who had once served in the French army and who was now with the Americans, came to tell him that the Vicomte de Mauroy and a number of other Frenchmen were leaving the United States, since they had not yet received the commissions Congress had promised them. De Kalb, however, had been confirmed as a major general and was staying on. Conway criticized De Kalb, Washington, and, in fact, almost everyone. But Lafayette detested intrigue and was determined not to become involved in personal feuds. He simply refused to listen to this gossip.

Although he was well treated by the Moravians, he longed to return to the army. He still walked with a limp; he could not put on his high boots. His wound bothered him, but inactivity bothered him more. So on October 18 he rejoined Washington's "family." The Commander-in-Chief received him affectionately. The entire American army was now interested in this young Frenchman who had been wounded while fighting at their side. They knew that he had left a charming wife and baby in France, and that another child was expected. They knew, also, that he was worried because he had received no news from home. When mail arrived from Benjamin Franklin in Paris, everyone hoped that finally there would be a letter for the Marquis de Lafayette.

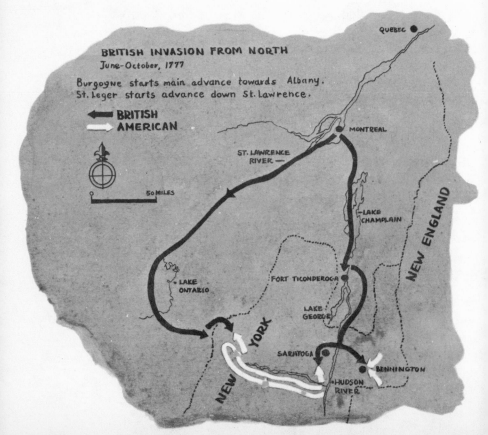

BRITISH INVASION FROM NORTH
June-October, 1777

Burgoyne starts main advance towards Albany.
St. Leger starts advance down St. Lawrence.

BRITISH
AMERICAN

50 MILES

QUEBEC

MONTREAL

ST. LAWRENCE RIVER —

LAKE CHAMPLAIN

NEW ENGLAND

LAKE ONTARIO

FORT TICONDEROGA

LAKE GEORGE

SARATOGA

BENNINGTON

HUDSON RIVER

NEW YORK

Good news was waiting for him when he rejoined the General Staff. In his drive down from Canada, the English general, Burgoyne, had been defeated at the Battle of Saratoga and surrendered his sword to the American general, Gates. It was a great victory for the Americans. Unfortunately, it resulted in complications. General Gates was very ambitious, and some of his friends — including the shifty Conway — tried to tempt him. They told him that he was just the man to replace Washington as commander-in-chief since he had won a great victory over the English, while Washington had suffered a series of defeats. In reality, Gates would have been a poor substitute, since Washington was a truly great man and Gates a mediocrity.

Lafayette soon began to feel restless and dissatisfied with his assignment in headquarters. He had not received the command he had been promised. He did not comprehend English well enough to understand the conversation of his comrades, and this made it difficult for him to work effectively with them. At Versailles, he had often

complained of the ceremonial pomp and the fri-
volity of the conversation. In camp, he suffered
rather from the excessive familiarity and the
general boredom. Sometimes, when he was depressed, he thought it might be better to return
to France rather than to vegetate uselessly in
America.

He talked to Washington about this idea.
Washington was worried. He was genuinely
fond of the young man, of whom he held a
high opinion. He feared, moreover, that Lafayette's return to France would make a bad impression in certain very influential circles, particularly since the Marquis had set out with such
enthusiasm. He wrote to John Hancock, the President of Congress:

"It appears to me, from a consideration of his
illustrious and important connections, the attach-
ment which he has manifested for our cause, and
the consequences which his return in disgust
might produce, that it will be advisable to gratify
him in his wishes . . ."

Since Hancock's reply was slow in arriving,

Lafayette asked permission to accompany General Greene, who was carrying on guerrilla warfare against the troops of General Cornwallis. Greene was glad to have Lafayette with him. The young officer immediately asked Greene to assign him to a reconnaissance mission to spy out the English positions. He still limped, for his wound was not completely healed. But Greene did not want to refuse, and granted him his wish.

Lafayette set out with a small group of French soldiers, reinforced by about 150 riflemen ("skillful combat men," notes Lafayette in his *Mémoires*, "who grew up on the wild frontier") and two pickets of militia, composed of some 75 men each. These 300 soldiers began their march toward Gloucester, New Jersey, to the accompaniment of fife and drum and in high good spirits. There the enemy was awaiting them. To make certain of the foe's position, the Marquis went forward alone on an exposed peninsula of land extending into the Delaware River. His friends, well hidden in the forest, called to him to come back. "They'll see you, General!"

But Lafayette *wanted* to be seen. With him, pride and personal honor were always more important than prudence. Finally, he agreed to withdraw. He had discovered that before him lay an advance post of some 400 Hessians equipped with cannon. He decided to launch a sudden attack. The Hessians were taken completely by surprise; they offered no resistance, and retreated to Gloucester in confusion. Lord Cornwallis thought he had the entire army of Greene to reckon with, and pushed into the forest with his grenadiers. In this operation, he lost 60 men.

The Americans were jubilant about this little victory, for their recent successes had been few and far between. This time Lafayette had actually earned the right to command a division. On the first of December, Congress passed a resolution that "General Washington be informed it is highly agreeable to Congress that the Marquis de Lafayette be appointed to the command of a division of the Continental Army." Washington, very satisfied, told Lafayette that he might take his choice among the available divisions. He settled on the Virginians.

Officers and men alike hailed his nomination with joy. Lafayette was so popular with everyone that his success caused no jealousy. He received letters of congratulation from every part of the country. He had become famous. His correspondents simply addressed their letters to "Monsieur le Marquis." Many of them did not know his name. Some were baffled by the pronunciation and spelled it "General de Fiat."

General Howe and Lord Cornwallis, uncertain of the strength of their adversary, decided to withdraw to Philadelphia. Washington made up his mind to set up winter quarters at Valley Forge, twenty-two miles away. Naturally, Lafayette, at the head of his division, followed him there. On the way, he received a letter from the old Maréchal de Noailles, his wife's grandfather, telling him that Adrienne was the mother of another daughter, Anastasie. The Maréchal, who had wanted a boy, commented acidly, "It's nothing to rejoice over."

That was not Lafayette's opinion, however. How much he wanted to hear directly from Adrienne! And how very long it seemed since he had received a letter.

6

From Valley Forge to Albany

THE WINTER of 1777–78 at Valley Forge was a terrible one for the American army. On their arrival, the soldiers, in order to protect themselves from the weather, felled trees to build log shelters. They had neither comfortable living quarters nor adequate defenses. After the soldiers constructed their huts they laid out rude streets. Material was lacking for roofs that would keep out rain and snow. The army was cold, miserable, underfed. How long would it last? Who could say?

The Virginia Division that Lafayette commanded was scarcely as large as a regiment in the French army. Many of the volunteers, at the end of their term of service, did not re-enlist; the

life was too hard. The army had no quartermaster
—each soldier had to provide for himself, supply
his own clothing and food. Often the army at
Valley Forge subsisted for an entire week without meat. Horses died of hunger. There was no
forage. Many soldiers lacked shoes, and the snow-
covered paths were stained with bloody foot-
prints. During the month of February some 4000
men were virtually confined to their miserable
huts because they had no winter clothing to wear.

If he had wished, Lafayette could have lived
comfortably in town, but he preferred to share
the hardships of his men. When he saw that they
were without shirts, he bought clothing for them
at his own expense. His men called him "the soldier's friend."

The situation of the Americans had never been
so desperate. The English had printed and dis-
tributed counterfeit dollars, and this astute operation had succeeded in devaluating the American
money and in spreading economic disorder. War
profiteers preferred to sell their goods to Lord
Howe who paid in gold rather than to the Amer-

icans at Valley Forge who paid in worthless paper.

By and large, however, the morale of the army was good. The soldiers made light of their misfortunes as they sang, "No pay, no clothes, no provisions, no rum."

This harsh school made a man of the young general. At scarcely twenty, he served a tough apprenticeship in the art of leadership. He wrote to the Duc d'Ayen: "I read, study, listen, and think, and while turning all this over in my mind, I try to formulate an over-all view of things that will remain true to common sense. I try not to say very much, in order not to say anything foolish — and I shall try to be very cautious in order not to *do* anything foolish . . . I do not believe that the desire for success and glory should endanger the safety of an entire army." And he added that for the moment he felt the Americans should remain on the defensive. Admirable wisdom for a man whose impulsive nature naturally encouraged him to take the offensive.

Lafayette's good sense was most useful to Washington. For it was he, a young foreigner, little more than a boy, who uncovered a plot against the Commander-in-Chief which, if it had succeeded, would have been fatal to the American cause.

The more he saw of this new country, the more convinced Lafayette became that Washington alone had the spirit that could lead the young nation to independence. But many Americans disagreed with him. Jealousy and intrigue were rampant everywhere — in Congress as well as in the army. Gates, the hero of Saratoga, was not at Valley Forge. With Conway, the Irishman (who had also become a general), he hatched plots to overthrow Washington. The friendship between Washington and Lafayette was an annoyance to them because of Lafayette's influence on French opinion. Consequently, they tried to turn "the Boy" (as they called him) against his commander-in-chief.

They invited the Marquis to come to see them in York, Pennsylvania. But he refused to leave his division. Every night, in the snow, he personally made the rounds to inspect the sentinels. When

Martha Washington wanted to send him parcels of food from Mount Vernon, he declined with thanks. He wanted to live in the manner of the common soldier. When Conway realized that Lafayette would not come to York, he himself went to Valley Forge to talk with the Marquis, and to play the role of the tempter.

"Why should you stay here, living in a tent in the snow, eating salt pork, when in Paris your wife and your children — who suffer from this long separation — are anxiously awaiting your

FROM VALLEY FORGE TO ALBANY | 87

return? Why not go home now and enjoy the prestige you have earned through your bravery and your military successes, instead of staying here in the mud of Valley Forge and running the risk of final defeat?"

In his conversation with the Marquis, Conway did not dare attack Washington directly. But back in York, the conspirators were bolder. There they planned between them to replace Washington by Gates who, according to their view, was "the only American general who has won a major battle in this whole war." A number of politicians journeyed to York to lend support to this project. The Adamses, who were very powerful, were openly hostile to Washington. John Adams, at the conclusion of a dinner, had even gone so far as to proclaim publicly, "This is my toast: to a short and violent war."

Washington replied to these attacks with great dignity. Doubtless he would have liked to point out to these gentlemen that it is easy to perform miracles of armchair strategy in the comfort of a well-heated room. They would have taken quite a different attitude if they were doing the fighting themselves, camping on bare, windswept heights, and sleeping in the snow.

Lafayette, in all his youth and candor, convinced of the purity and the nobility of all those engaged in the struggle for liberty, refused for a long time to believe in the existence of these base maneuvers. But finally he saw an exchange of letters between Gates and Conway in which Washington was treated with impudence and contempt. Indignant, he immediately tried to see the Commander-in-Chief, but Washington was busy. So Lafayette wrote him a letter:

"Lay aside for an instant that personal modesty which — I beg you to excuse me, sir — is often excessive, and you will see clearly that if your country lost you as its leader, no one could hold the army together and the whole revolutionary movement would be dead within six months. Some people, who are completely lacking in military judgment, have taken it upon themselves to criticize your actions and to make absurd comparisons. For them, General Gates can do no

wrong and they imagine that an immediate offensive would result in an easy victory . . . I so wish
that you could make them promise to stop their
intriguing or, at least, to give an appearance of
being united until the time when their personal
quarrels will no longer be a danger."

It was clear from his letter that this young man
had more statesmanship than many diplomats
twice his age. Washington reassured him.

". . . We must not, in so great a contest, expect
to meet with nothing but sunshine. I have no
doubt that everything happens for the best, that
we shall triumph over all our misfortunes, and
in the end be happy."

On January 22, Congress decided to create an
army to invade Canada and to put it under the
command of Lafayette. This was a new move
on the part of Washington's enemies, designed to
create jealousy between him and Lafayette. They
thought they could win the Marquis by offering
him a post comparable to that of the Commander-
in-Chief. Lafayette promptly received news from
Congress confirming his appointment, together

with orders to proceed to Albany to receive instructions. Washington gravely handed the envelope to the young man without a word of comment.

The reaction of the Marquis showed how completely loyal he was. He replied to the representatives of Congress who were then in camp, "I shall never accept any command independent of that of General Washington. I can accept this appointment only in the capacity of an officer of his staff detached for a temporary assignment, and it is to him that I shall address my reports." Because Congress needed Lafayette, they were obliged to accept his qualifying conditions.

Since he could now assume command of the Canadian expedition without betraying the confidence of the General, Lafayette proceeded happily toward Albany. He was jubilant in the hope of reconquering Canada from the English and of returning this territory to the King of France in the name of the young American republic. For Lafayette, it would be a dream come true. France would be justly proud of him and truly grateful for what he had accomplished; strong bonds of friendship would be created between his own country and America; and even the Queen would have to admit that the young man who had been so clumsy a dancer had become a distinguished soldier.

The trip to Albany was slow and difficult. Lafayette had approximately 400 miles to travel, partly on horseback, partly in horse-drawn sleighs, and was often obliged to cross rivers

choked with ice. As he pushed ahead into the wilderness, he was thinking seriously. Would he be able to accomplish this mission? He was a young officer with but little experience, suddenly called upon to lead an invading army. What a heavy responsibility! How would he feed his men in this frozen wilderness? The invasion might easily end in disaster. But it was too late now to refuse the command. "My honor is at stake." That was always the first consideration with Lafayette.

Naturally he had written to his wife to tell her about his promotion. "This immense territory of Canada is under the yoke of the English. They maintain a fleet there, together with an army, and ports of entry. As general of the Army of the North, with a force of three thousand men, I have been given the mission of inflicting what damage I can on the English . . . This is an enormous task, and the resources at our disposition are very modest . . . Besides, it's not easy to take command of an army at the age of twenty."

Nevertheless, until he reached Albany, he was

full of hope. There he found Conway, who immediately told him that an invasion of Canada was
out of the question. At first Lafayette protested
violently. Then he consulted other military leaders. They were in agreement that it would be
madness. First, instead of the 3000 men Lafayette had been promised, there were but 1200.
These, moreover, were unequipped, even for a
summer campaign, and they had not been paid
for many months.

Lafayette was desperate. The whole assignment began to appear incredible. He had been
offered a major command; he had announced the
good news to his family. Now all his friends in
Europe knew about it, and apparently nothing
was to come of all this huffing and puffing! He
wrote to Washington to tell him of "the humiliating and ridiculous situation" in which he had been
placed. "People will certainly make fun of us.
I admit, General, that I cannot control my feelings when my honor and reputation are at stake
. . . I assure you, dear and venerated friend, that
I have never been as unhappy as at this moment."

He gradually realized that he had been tricked and that his "promotion" was only a maneuver in the Gates-Conway conspiracy. They had wanted to create bad feeling between him and Washington, and, at the same time, make him look ridiculous. He suffered bitterly, but was astute enough not to complain publicly. However, so that his long trip should not be completely useless, he continued from Albany up the Mohawk Valley in order to negotiate with the Indian tribes of that area. The "Boy" succeeded very well with these plume-bedecked warriors. He gave them French coins of gold to wear like medals around their necks. He smoked the peace pipe with them to seal a treaty of friendship. Congress approved his attitude. And Washington soothed his pride by writing that he was in no way dishonored if he was "unable to conquer the seasons." At last Congress authorized him to return to Valley Forge, to join the Commander-in-Chief for whom he had such deep devotion.

7

Lafayette and the Franco-American Alliance

IT WAS NOT UNTIL SPRING that Lafayette returned
to Valley Forge. The army, cheered by the sun,
better fed, and newly reorganized, was far more
hopeful for the future. On May 2, 1778, Simeon
Deane (brother of Silas Deane who had originally
commissioned Lafayette in Paris) arrived on a
French frigate. He brought good news. The King
of France had signed a treaty of alliance with
America. As soon as it was signed and sealed,
Franklin and Deane had hastened to the Duc
d'Ayen's to offer their congratulations to the wife
of the Marquis de Lafayette. Voltaire himself had
expressed the desire to make her acquaintance
and had said, "I wish to pay homage to the wife

of the hero of the New World; I only hope to live long enough to hail him as the liberator of the Old."

All this praise sounded singularly sweet to Lafayette after the criticism he had received since leaving France and, most recently, in Albany! How proud Adrienne and his relatives would be! He mounted a horse, galloped to Washington's headquarters, and kissed the commander on both cheeks! This must have been rather overwhelming to an American general. Washington, however, smiled graciously and warmly congratulated his young friend.

"You have done more than anyone else to bring about this great event," he said.

When Lafayette read the note of the French government to the British Cabinet stating that the Americans had "become independent by their Declaration of the 4th of July, 1776," he smiled to himself and thought, one day the French themselves will remember that idealistic principle.

The following days were filled with celebrations. Banquets were organized. Bonfires were lighted. Everywhere the French flag, with its fleur-de-lis, flew beside the Stars and Stripes. Lafayette wore a white sash across his American uniform. He had reason to be proud and happy. Everyone applauded him as the Frenchman who had led France into the camp of Liberty. And now Lafayette had the additional satisfaction of knowing that he was fighting for his own country as well as for the American republic.

To dignify the occasion, Washington ordered a full-dress review of the army. Cannons were

fired, while the soldiers shouted, "Long live the King of France! Long live the United States!"

There was a single dark cloud on the blue horizon. Lafayette had just learned that Henriette, his older daughter, had died. He imagined how grief-stricken his wife must be—a grief intensified by their separation. Public duty, however, must take precedence over personal sorrow.

What would the English do? Some predicted that because of the intervention of France, the redcoats would evacuate Philadelphia. The time

had come for the Americans to take the offensive and to give the enemy no quarter. Washington decided to put Lafayette in command of 2000 picked men and to send him on a reconnaissance mission. This was an important assignment. Several generals had requested it. But Washington gave it to Lafayette, a young man in whom he had increasing confidence. Through their spies, the English soon learned that Lafayette was in command of the troops opposing them. In the past, they had always refused to take "the Boy" seriously; but he now was beginning to assume ominous importance. Since Lafayette was foolish enough to put his head in the lion's mouth, they were determined to capture him and to send him back to Paris as they might a naughty, runaway child. They would make him a laughingstock!

The British prepared an expedition to foster their plans. General Clinton was in command. And, although he had just been recalled to London, General Howe decided to postpone his departure and take part in the scheme—"just for the fun of it." Admiral Howe, his brother, ordered a frigate to be ready to return the famous prisoner to Europe. A banquet was organized to celebrate the capture of the young Marquis, and General Howe went so far as to send elegant invitations to the Philadelphia belles inscribed: "To meet M. de Lafayette."

Two separate columns — 8000 men and 15 pieces of field artillery — were dispatched to surround the Marquis' men. They were instructed to join forces behind the Americans. Suddenly, when least expected, Lafayette discovered that the redcoats (or "the lobsters," as the Americans called them) were rapidly advancing. This news might easily have flustered him, but during his months in America he had learned much about strategy. There was only one way to escape — by the river, which he could cross at Matson's Ford. He dispatched most of his men to that point. At the same time, in order to divert the attention of the enemy, he led an attack in the opposite direction, thus drawing the British away from the major American force.

It was Lafayette's good fortune that the English general, Grant, who was supposed to hold the ford, had stopped at the Broadaxe Inn for breakfast — an excellent and hearty breakfast! Therefore he was late. When Lafayette attacked, Grant lost additional time in countering this feint. Then Lafayette retreated silently and rapidly toward the river crossing where he rejoined his troops. In the course of this operation, only six or seven casualties were incurred. When the two columns of "lobsters" joined forces and "closed the net" according to plan, they were surprised to find it empty. Lafayette had disappeared, and the banquet "to meet him" had to be canceled.

A few days later, Lafayette might have won another major triumph at the Battle of Monmouth if he had not, through courtesy, relinquished his command to General Charles Lee. The latter, because of treason or incompetence, allowed victory to slip through his fingers.

Soon after, the Marquis learned that a French fleet, commanded by Charles d'Estaing, who, like himself, hailed from the province of Auvergne, had anchored at the mouth of the Delaware River.

The Comte Charles d'Estaing was (again like Lafayette) a liberal. He had long been a soldier and had campaigned in India against the English before the French King had named him admiral. A fiery, violent personality, he was overjoyed to be in command of the fleet sent to fight the English in America. Unhappily, the transatlantic voyage had been difficult. It had lasted for nearly three months. Water had been in short supply, there was insufficient food, and many of the crew fell ill with scurvy.

Consequently, D'Estaing had arrived too late to blockade the English fleet in Philadelphia before its withdrawal to New York. D'Estaing set out for New York in his flagship, the *Languedoc*, but discovered that the draft of his ships prevented them from entering the harbor. What could he do? Without proper anchorage, he was forced to cruise in Long Island Sound and in the waters off Rhode Island. The English had several frigates in this area, as well as some 4000 soldiers stationed in Rhode Island. Washington instructed General Sullivan — under whom Lafayette was then serving—to launch a major attack on these forces with the support of the French fleet.

Lafayette, although very happy about the arrival of his compatriots, was also worried. After all, he had left France without proper authorization. How would a French admiral receive him? Naturally he boarded the *Languedoc* with mixed emotions. He was relieved when the Admiral immediately flung his arms about him in a warm embrace.

"You, Lafayette, will command the landing party of French infantry," D'Estaing announced to him. The young Marquis was overcome with joy. He had never dreamed that he would be a commander of both French and American troops.

"I would rather be a common soldier in the French army than a general anywhere else," he had said.

Alas! When two nations are striving to cooperate, it is not always easy to settle questions of prestige. Very soon the French and Americans were quarreling. The French fleet needed drinking water, fresh vegetables, and meat. The Americans, because of their faulty organization, were often unable to furnish these supplies when they were required. And they complained that the French took a very long time to get into action. The French career officers, moreover, were rather contemptuous of these volunteer soldiers, who often lacked proper uniforms. "It's not an army," they exclaimed. "It's nothing but a band of Tartars."

Poor Lafayette found himself in a difficult position. The French treated him as though he were an American; the Americans, who had considered him one of them, now saw him among his fellow countrymen and realized that he remained very French. Both sides criticized him — the Americans because he was too French, the French because he was too American. Sullivan did not want Lafayette to command the French troops. He wanted to lead the landings in Rhode Island himself. Lafayette insisted that this would be an affront to the honor of France.

Finally it was decided that both French and American troops would land at the same time.

But Sullivan did not keep his bargain. An eye-witness to these events wrote, "it was like a group of jealous women fiercely squabbling about who was going to lead the dance"! Nevertheless, D'Estaing forgot his understandable resentment and went to the rescue of Sullivan when, after the fog lifted, the British fleet appeared. Admiral d'Estaing fought the whole day. Toward evening, when the enemy had turned to flee and he was in hot pursuit, a terrible storm came up and severely damaged several of the French ships. The Admiral had to take his fleet to Boston to repair the havoc.

But this led Sullivan and his officers to believe that they had been abandoned by their allies, and they cried treason. Because of his position, Lafayette considered it his duty to try to smooth over the difficulties, thus preventing a break in relations. The people of Boston, excited by false rumors, talked of closing the port to the French fleet. The American generals drew up a censure of D'Estaing which Lafayette refused to sign. Sullivan, exasperated and unreasonable, included

the phrase "Our allies have abandoned us" in the order of the day to the army. Lafayette demanded that this be stricken out. He refused to listen to criticism of the French fleet and preferred to sacrifice his popularity rather than leave any shadow of doubt upon his loyalty to his own country.

He hurried to Boston where Admiral d'Estaing proved to him that there was certainly no treason, for he could not have acted otherwise. Returning to Rhode Island, which had been virtually evacuated by the Americans, Lafayette covered the retreat of the last troops, showing such courage in combat that even Sullivan apologized to him and cited him in his dispatches. Washington wrote a fine letter to Admiral d'Estaing. The French fleet sailed for the West Indies. Everything appeared more serene. Lafayette, however, was inconsolable. When the French had arrived, he had had such great hopes!

Once again fired with feverish enthusiasm, he began to make ambitious plans — rather impractical ones, to be sure — to reconquer his fame and glory.

In his fatherly wisdom, Washington realized how dangerous this impatience was. He wrote to Lafayette suggesting that he should return for a time to France, visit his wife and his friends, and appear at Court again.

Lafayette certainly longed to see his family and his homeland. But what would people think? Would they not say that he had abandoned the Americans? Washington advised him to ask for leave, with the understanding that he would soon return to America to resume his command. While in France, he could do much for the American cause. Congress not only granted him his leave, but gave him a vote of thanks and placed a handsome vessel, the *Alliance*, at his complete disposal for the trip back to France.

8
Back to France

I<small>T WAS A</small> rough crossing. Near Newfoundland, a terrible storm broke out. In the tempest, the masts snapped off and the *Alliance* sprang a leak. Lafayette, who had been ailing before he left, suffered miserably from seasickness and could not leave his cabin. Occasionally, he would send a French friend, Pontgibaud, on deck to reconnoiter. The reports he gave were never very encouraging.

"Think of it," Lafayette said. "That I should come out here and go through all I have gone through only to end up as food for the cod!"

After the storm at sea, there was another kind of storm on board the ship. It had been difficult to assemble a crew, so a number of deserters from the English navy had been engaged. One day, as they were approaching the Continent, one of the American sailors came to Lafayette and asked to speak to him confidentially. He said that George III had announced that if English deserters mutinied and captured a ship and brought it safely to port in England, they would not only be pardoned but would receive a reward. Having heard of this offer, the English deserters on board were planning to revolt, take over the ship, and deliver Lafayette to the enemy.

When threatened by danger, Lafayette always took prompt and decisive action. He called a secret meeting of the French and the American sailors and had them indicate the leaders of the conspiracy. He then cut the ropes of their hammocks as they slept. Thus entangled, thirty-three of them were put in irons. After this episode, all was calm on board, and the *Alliance* safely reached the port of Brest on February 6.

Here Lafayette leaped into a stagecoach and left immediately for Versailles, where he saw his cousin, the Prince de Poix, who was Captain of the Guards. The prince had great influence at the Palace and succeeded in obtaining interviews for Lafayette with the ministers Maurepas and Vergennes. They received him cordially, and he hurried on to Paris.

No one at the Noailles mansion knew he had returned. He asked the servants first to tell his mother-in-law, the Duchesse d'Ayen, because he did not wish to upset his wife, who was still in delicate health. The Duchesse appeared at once, embraced him, and sent for Adrienne who came, trembling with joy, to fling herself into her husband's arms. They both told him how proud they were of him. They had never lost faith! But one danger still remained. In spite of his heroic deeds in America, he was a French officer who had left the service of the King without permission. Would he be punished as a deserter? Would he be sent to the Bastille?

Perhaps he might have been punished, at least for form's sake, had he not been so universally popular. As it was, his return aroused so much enthusiasm that the government did not dare to treat him severely. For a pleasant eight days, in his own home, he was placed under house arrest guarded by the Maréchal de Noailles. Officially he was permitted to see only members of his family, but since he was related to half the French aristocracy, and since Franklin was allowed to visit, the punishment was not too hard to bear.

He had brought enthusiastic letters from Congress commending him to the American representatives in Paris and to the King of France. He immediately wrote a personal letter full of contrition to his King, expressing regret for having flouted the wishes of his government. He explained that his strong emotions had prevailed over his better judgment. In the future, he said, he desired to serve his King in any country, and remained the monarch's "humble and obedient servant." His grandfather and his father-in-law had each assisted and advised to help produce this model of a courtly letter.

It had the desired effect. Louis XVI promptly invited Lafayette to Versailles to be forgiven. He was fatherly and affectionate. He murmured a few words about discipline and the duty of an officer, and then began to question him avidly about America, and especially about Washington. The young man was eager to talk on the subject, and his conversation proved very interesting to the King.

Even the Queen was anxious to see him. In the past, she had never cared much for him, but she realized that he had now become the idol of the Court. On his first visit, a number of ladies rushed up to him and threw themselves into his arms. In

Paris, whenever he appeared in public, people burst into spontaneous applause. One evening at the Comédie Française, when the actors learned that he was present, they added to the perform- ance eight lines — not very good ones, alas — especially in his honor, and the entire audience rose to applaud. It was said that Marie Antoinette was so eager to see him that, oblivious of the rain, she rushed out to meet him on his first visit to Versailles. Of course, there was not a word of truth in it. Nevertheless she had received him very graciously and had obtained for him the command of a famous regiment, the King's Dra- goons, and the rank of *mestre-de-camp* (equiv- alent to that of colonel). His fortunes were certainly improving. Two years before, he had been considered clumsy and maladroit, and no one paid much attention to him. Now everyone sought him out; people crowded around him. "That's what a little courage and perseverance can do for you," he told himself.

Success in society did not really interest him, however. He wanted to meet ministers, not beau-

tiful ladies. He had returned to France partly
to see his family, but principally to obtain the
active support of the King for the American cause.
He had ambitious plans, and he discussed them
all day long — sometimes with the ministers
Maurepas and Vergennes; sometimes with Benjamin Franklin; sometimes with liberal young
noblemen like the Prince de Poix, the Comte de
Ségur, or the Vicomte de Noailles, who shared
his ideas. His father-in-law, the Duc d'Ayen, who
had criticized him so bitterly when he left for
America, now wished to go there himself!

The ministers with whom he conferred were
not completely opposed to sending a small armed
force to help the United States. Nevertheless,
they still raised certain objections. They pointed
out that Admiral d'Estaing had not been well
received. The Americans, it appeared, had almost
resented his arrival. Moreover, it seemed difficult
to deal with these Americans since they could not
agree even among themselves. Congress itself
was divided. Right here in Paris there were two
hostile groups of American representatives, each

claiming that the other was acting without authority. Franklin had constant difficulties with
John Adams and Arthur Lee.

The Marquis continued to repeat from morning till night the obvious truth that there were
always hostile cliques everywhere, but that Washington stood above all these quarrels and was a
genuinely great man, and that Franklin was the
sole accredited representative of the United States
in France.

While awaiting a decision on the question of
sending French troops to the support of Washington, Lafayette proposed a number of other
plans: Why not invade Canada and restore this
vast territory to the French Empire? Or why not
send an expedition by sea to invade England?
This could be done without officially involving the
French government simply by making ships available to the American freebooter John Paul Jones,
who was then living in Paris. Or why not foment
an uprising in Ireland against the British?

In the midst of all this, the Marquis was ordered to take command of his regiment, which

was stationed in the little town of Saint Jean d'Angely. Think of sending him to vegetate in such an out-of-the-way place, after he had distinguished himself in front-line combat! He felt that he was being wasted, and wrote to Vergennes, not officially, but as a friend: "I love the military life more than anything else in the world, and I honestly believe that I was born for it. I wish to serve my country to the very best of my ability, and I am anxiously awaiting word that I may be the first to land on the English coast."

Suddenly he received an urgent order from the Court to return immediately to Versailles. From there, he was to proceed to Le Havre to be second in command of a joint French and Spanish expeditionary force to invade England. The adventure was badly organized, however, and the Spanish fleet never appeared. People said ironically that M. de Sartines, the incompetent French Minister of the Navy, "had a watch that was six months slow." The whole idea of an invasion of England was abandoned.

Still undaunted, Lafayette immediately revived

the idea of sending a French expeditionary force to America. He asked for only 4000 men, but he stipulated that he should be in sole command.

"They will say, Monsieur le Comte," he wrote to Vergennes, "that the French will be badly received in that country . . . I cannot deny that Americans are sometimes difficult to get along with, especially for Frenchmen, but if I have charge of things, I am willing to wager my head that I will be able to avoid all difficulties and our troops will be received perfectly." It was only necessary to choose officers who could stand hardship and would be satisfied to do without amusements, girls, and letters from home for many long months.

And what about the young Marquis? Could he bring himself to leave his gentle Adrienne once again? She was still in poor health and was now expecting her third baby; and she was only nineteen.

It was true that suffering and responsibility had matured her, but she hated the stern fact that her beloved husband must leave again for war.

Nevertheless, she understood and approved his love of glory and his devotion to the cause of liberty. She was at Le Havre with him when Franklin's little grandson presented Lafayette with a sword which the American Congress had ordered from one of the best jewelers of Paris. It was set with diamonds and had been designed by Franklin himself. Engraved upon it was Lafayette's motto, *Cur non* (Why not?), a portrayal of America breaking her chains, and scenes from the principal battles in which Lafayette had taken part.

In December, the Marquise de Lafayette gave birth to a boy, who was christened George Washington.

The French Minister of Foreign Affairs, Vergennes, was by now convinced of the necessity of sending an expeditionary force to America, but Maurepas, the Prime Minister, still had to be won over. Lafayette, with the help of Vergennes, wrote him a long, well-reasoned report which succeeded in gaining his cooperation.

A French force would be sent. Six million pounds would be loaned to the Americans for the purchase of arms and uniforms.

Who would be in command? Lafayette rea-
soned, "I should be, because the Americans know
me. If not, I must leave France well in advance
of the army." Military tradition, as usual, won
the day over realistic political considerations. The
French generals were scandalized at the idea
of accepting orders from a young "upstart" of
twenty-two. Consequently, the King named the
Comte de Rochambeau, a lieutenant general of
great experience, to command the expedition.
However, Lafayette would precede the troops
to announce to Washington the success of his
mission.

Before leaving, Lafayette proudly and openly
donned the uniform of major general of the
American army and went to keep his audience
with the King. Then on the 11th of March, 1780,
he said farewell, embraced his tearful wife,
boarded the French frigate, *Hermione*, and once
again sailed off across the stormy Atlantic for
America.

9

The Arrival of Rochambeau

WHEN THE *Hermione* arrived in Boston and the authorities learned that Lafayette was aboard, they asked him to delay his landing in order that the welcoming committee might have time to prepare a big reception in his honor. Naturally he complied. And he immediately wrote to Washington: "I am back, dear General, and have important news which I have been authorized to communicate to you alone."

This news, of course, concerned the sending of French aid and was to be kept secret to avoid alerting the English fleet.

Next day, Boston gave Lafayette an enthusiastic welcome. No one had known that the Marquis was really coming back. He always loved dramatic effects — and he certainly had achieved one. The cannons thundered, the bells tolled, bonfires were lighted. As for Washington, when he received Lafayette's letter, he was so deeply moved that tears came to his eyes. This show of emotion, for a man who always tried to conceal his feelings, was proof of the deep affection he had for the young Frenchman. Washington replied, asking Lafayette to rejoin him in Morristown, New Jersey, as soon as possible.

Lafayette arrived there on the 10th of May, happy to be with "his family" once again. In private, he told Washington his heartening news: that France was sending troops and money. Washington was overjoyed, but revealed that this eleventh-hour help came just in time; the situation had never been so serious. Congress was wasting precious time in fruitless bickering. No money was available. The army — unpaid, unfed, and without proper clothing — had dwindled to 6000 men. In the South, a combined French-American force had been beaten at Savannah.

Clinton and Cornwallis had reconquered South
Carolina, where Lafayette had formerly landed.
Charleston had been retaken by the English, who
were supported there by a "fifth column" of
American Tories.

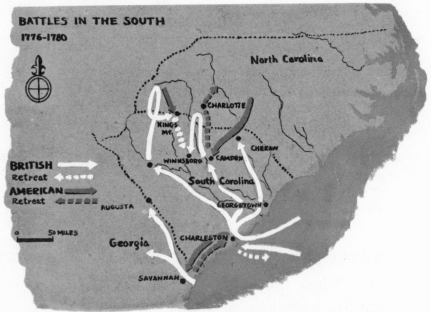

BATTLES IN THE SOUTH
1776-1780

North Carolina

CHARLOTTE

KINGS MT.

CHERAW

WINNSBORO   CAMDEN

BRITISH
Retreat

AMERICAN
Retreat

South Carolina

GEORGETOWN

AUGUSTA

0   50 MILES

Georgia   CHARLESTON

SAVANNAH

Lafayette's spirits sank. Would he be obliged
to greet Rochambeau and his men on their arrival
with this humiliating news? The situation must
be changed at any cost. Washington decided to
send Lafayette to Philadelphia to stir up Con-

gress. But in what manner? He could not reveal the impending arrival of French troops. Fortunately, the English now announced in their American newspapers that they had learned of the French expedition, so overnight it ceased to be a secret. Actually, it was even claimed that the French were heading for Newport, Rhode Island, which was in fact the truth.

In July, the fleet commanded by Admiral Ternay landed Rochambeau's army at Newport. The crossing had taken seventy days. Washington sent a letter by Lafayette to Rochambeau recommending this young friend in whom he had such complete confidence. "All the information he gives, and all the propositions he makes, I entreat you to consider as coming from me. I request you will settle all arrangements whatsoever with him."

Lafayette was delighted. Rochambeau was not.

Rochambeau was a seasoned commander, fifty-five years old, who had had a great deal of combat experience. In order to avoid friction, he had consented to serve under the command of Washington. But he wanted to receive instructions directly from his chief. To have them transmitted by a stripling of twenty-two — that was too much!

Lafayette explained that Washington wished the French and American troops to take the offensive and lay siege to New York. The old campaigner listened to all this with a mixture of amusement and suspicion. The young man was too enthusiastic — and enthusiasm is not a military virtue. Before launching any offensive, Rochambeau wanted to be absolutely certain that he had naval superiority.

"I shan't make a move unless I am sure that we command the sea."

As a matter of fact, the English had naval superiority and were to keep it until the second French squadron arrived. Moreover, Rochambeau had decided to talk things over directly with Washington. Consequently, during his first trip to Newport, Lafayette accomplished little except to see his friends in the French expeditionary force. He had a great many of them. The proudest names of France had crossed the ocean to seek fame in America. There were Lafayette's brother-in-law, Noailles, and a host of others — Custine, Montmorency, Charlus, Lauzun, Damas. These dashing young officers had quickly become very popular in Rhode Island. In fact, certain suspicious fathers in Newport were afraid that they were becoming altogether *too* popular. It was said that the Duc de Lauzun tried to flirt with every woman he met. But Rochambeau preached a stern lesson to his troops, and after that the army — officers and men alike — behaved admirably. There was no pillaging; every chicken, every apple was promptly paid for. The Puritan population was favorably impressed by these handsome, well-dressed officers who had such excellent discipline and who paid their debts in gold.

But the impetuous Lafayette did not think that the army had come all the way from France merely to dance with the pretty girls of Newport. In a letter, addressed jointly to Rochambeau and to Ternay, he outlined in precise order the plans of General Washington for an attack on New York. He concluded: "I assure you, gentlemen, in my own name, that this campaign is important and urgent and that even the reinforcements that may be sent from France next year will not be able to undo the damage caused by our present inaction."

The letter really annoyed Rochambeau. He answered sharply that he had already written to Washington explaining his position. "Consequently," he informed Lafayette, "I shall await *his* orders, hoping that he will be kind enough to grant me a personal interview." Evidently Rochambeau thought that more could be accomplished in fifteen minutes' conversation than with so many dispatches.

The Marquis' note had implied that the French troops in Rhode Island were doing nothing for the American cause. Rochambeau's reply put the facts in better perspective. The powerful, well-disciplined French force exercised a deterrent influence on the enemy simply by its presence. He added, "I fear these Savannahs and other such actions, of which I have seen so many in my life. There is a principle in war, as in geometry — *vis unita fortior* (a united force is stronger)."

Lafayette had the intelligence to understand that he had offended Rochambeau and wrote him a personal letter that was both friendly and modest. "I give you my word of honor, I thought I was only doing my duty in writing to you as I did . . . If I have offended you, I ask your pardon for two reasons, the first because of the affection that I have for you, and the second because my intention is to do here what you wish . . ."

Rochambeau was touched: "My dear Marquis, allow me to reply to you as a father would reply to a son for whom he has an infinite affection and esteem . . . If I pointed out to you (very gently) what displeased me in your last communication, it was because I understood that your ardor had prevailed over the wisdom of your judgment . . . It is still Old Father Rochambeau who speaks to his dear son Lafayette whom he loves, and will continue to love and esteem until his last breath."

Washington felt that there would be an explosion sooner or later if he did not separate Lafayette and Rochambeau. He had received disappointing news from the South where the too-famous Gates had been beaten by Cornwallis at Camden, and where De Kalb, Lafayette's first comrade-in-arms, had been killed. A "summit conference" was necessary in order to arrive at certain basic decisions. It was agreed that Washington and Rochambeau should meet in Hartford. A number of French officers accompanied Rochambeau to the conference. They looked forward to meeting Washington and were much impressed by his simplicity and dignity.

The discussion took place in an atmosphere of mutual courtesy. But Washington was quite aware that Rochambeau accepted him as commander-in-chief simply as a matter of form, as a polite fiction. However, he had no intention of making a military move if he were not personally convinced that he had a sufficient force at his disposition. It was agreed that an envoy would be sent to France to request more money, more men, and more ships. For the moment, the second French contingent was still at Brest, bottled up by the English fleet.

On his return from this conference, Washington learned of the treason of General Benedict Arnold. Arnold, after secret meetings with the British spy, Major André, had agreed to deliver to the enemy the Hudson River defenses that he was pledged to maintain. Lafayette was a member of the court-martial which condemned André to death after his capture inside the American lines. Lafayette could never forget this episode. He was filled with pity for the young officer who paid with his life for having done his duty. He remained in his room all day on October 2, when André was hanged.

Winter was setting in. The campaign was finished for that year. His friends Noailles, Lauzun, Damas, and Charlus invited him to come to Newport to pass the time with them and their girls. But Lafayette was not in the mood for parties. Washington had given him the command of a light-artillery brigade, and he was busy fitting it out with the equipment which he had brought from France. He had purchased for his

officers handsome helmets decorated with plumes of black and red. He was determined to have the best-armed and best-trained unit in the American army.

His friends often came to camp to see him and he took them visiting in Philadelphia. They were very well received; many dinners and banquets were given for them. Noailles and Damas were continuously occupied dancing with the prettiest belles in town. Lafayette, however, was more interested in talking with members of Congress.

He was worried about an anti-French minority bent on recalling Franklin from his post in Paris and making peace with England. Hence, it was more essential than ever to obtain fresh reinforcements from France. The decision was made to send young John Laurens, the son of Henry Laurens, President of Congress, to Paris. Lafayette provided him with a letter for Adrienne. The Marquis summed up the situation for his wife, then concluded:

"I was about to close this letter, but before I seal it, I must tell you once again of my love for you. General Washington was very happy when I gave him your message. He asks me to give you his most affectionate greetings — and to little George as well. He was very touched that we have named our son after him. We often speak together of you and of our little family. Adieu, adieu."

He was depressed sometimes when he thought of Adrienne. And yet for what reason? Was he not storing up for his children, and for their children as well, a glory that would be timeless?

10

THE YEAR 1781 began badly. In the South, General Cornwallis was still advancing. The traitor, Benedict Arnold, was in Virginia leading British troops. The French remained in Rhode Island, and the Americans continued to complain that their allies were giving no assistance. Lafayette, with 1200 men, had been sent by Washington to harry the enemy in Virginia.

It was a hard assignment for a young general of little experience to be matched against such old campaigners as Arnold and Cornwallis. Lafayette had hoped that some top French officers would accompany him, but they were weary of hearing the Americans praise Lafayette. So often they had been told, "How lucky you are to be a countryman of the hero Lafayette!" The French frequently wished they might reply: "Well, he isn't the only hero!" Their reaction was understandable.

The Marquis was also very much concerned about his own soldiers. Lacking shoes and sufficient clothing, they were deserting in increasing numbers, despite all that he tried to do for them. One day he called them together.

"I am not forcing any of you to follow me on this campaign in Virginia, for the dangers are great. It is unnecessary to desert; whoever wants to stay here in winter quarters need only ask me to have permission to do so. Let him who loves me follow me."

This short speech produced good results. Not one soldier took advantage of the offer, and there were no more desertions.

While passing through Baltimore, Lafayette appealed to the wealthy citizens for help. They donated 10,000 pounds to buy the shoes, clothing, and supplies that were so desperately needed, and groups of ladies banded together to make shirts for the men. By the end of March, Lafayette had arrived in Virginia. Arnold sent him a letter concerning the exchange of prisoners. The Marquis refused to open it, stating that he would be prepared to deal with any other English officer, but not with Arnold. Washington approved his stand.

Cornwallis presently joined forces with Arnold. Virginia was becoming an important theater of operations, since there was virtually no fighting in the North. Cornwallis did not take his inexperienced opponent very seriously, for he was certain that he could trap him easily.

"The boy cannot escape me," he boasted.

Even Lafayette was a little intimidated. He wrote to his brother-in-law, Noailles, not to judge him too severely if he failed to make a good showing. The difference in the size of the armies was immense and the difficulties indescribable.

But "the Boy" had learned much concerning military strategy. He was no longer carried away by his impulses. Instead of attacking Cornwallis immediately, he astutely retreated, by devious twists and turns, until he was reinforced by three Pennsylvania regiments. Then it was Cornwallis' turn to retreat, and he withdrew rapidly, abandoning Richmond. Lafayette soon discovered that the English forces had taken positions at the port of Yorktown.

Why? It seems that Cornwallis was so ordered by his commander-in-chief, Clinton, who, from the vantage point of New York, was watching the movements of the French in Rhode Island. Cornwallis had begged Clinton to join forces with him in the South and conclude the war there. But in vain. Clinton did not want Cornwallis to receive too much credit for the final victory. Besides, he feared what Rochambeau might do. As a matter of fact, at this very moment, Washington and Rochambeau were secretly preparing a plan for an all-out attack.

Rochambeau had always said, "Not a move without naval superiority." Now, for the time being, this superiority was within his grasp. There was a French fleet in the West Indies, under the command of Admiral de Grasse. It could, if neces-

sary, sail north for a few weeks, blockade Chesapeake Bay, and prevent Cornwallis from escaping
by sea. At the same time, Washington and
Rochambeau could hurry down to Virginia and
join Lafayette for an assault on Yorktown. They
thought in this way they could capture the entire
army of Cornwallis. However, to prevent Clinton
and his fleet from sailing to Yorktown, they pre-
tended to be preparing an attack on New York
City.

Lafayette, in Virginia, knew nothing of these
plans, and was becoming more and more worried.
He knew that Washington had praised him highly
for this campaign. He had been able to trick one
of the best of the English generals into pursuing
him, had managed to elude him and then to
corner him at Yorktown. It was a master stroke.
But with no news from the North, Lafayette was
uneasy. He wanted either to return to Washington's headquarters or else to join the French
forces. Washington slipped mysterious allusions
into his letters concerning "a major operation" in

the South, but what operation? Time hung heavy on Lafayette's hands.

Finally, a courier brought word from Washington. Admiral de Grasse had left Santo Domingo with a fleet of 25 or 30 vessels with detachments of land forces on board. They were sailing toward Chesapeake Bay. Lafayette was instructed to establish liaison with the Admiral while awaiting the arrival of reinforcements from the North. Immediately everything was clear. Without doubt, Washington himself and Rochambeau would soon be arriving! Now Lafayette was more than happy to remain in Virginia.

To his wife he wrote: "It really wasn't sensible to entrust such an important command to me. If I had failed, people would have said that such partiality was blindness . . . But I am sure that you were hopeful, dear one, that a man could not be clumsy in every field of endeavor." This last was obviously an allusion to his shortcomings as a courtier, as a dancer, and as a hunter—shortcomings of which his wife was tenderly aware.

Now she could be even prouder of her general.

The plan worked out wonderfully well. Clinton, when he saw the French troops from Rhode Island advancing on New York, believed that he would shortly be attacked. Admiral de Grasse arrived near Yorktown on schedule and landed 3000 superbly trained and well-equipped troops under the command of the Marquis de Saint-Simon. Lafayette joined forces with them, taking pains to see that his own troops looked as smart and well clad as possible. Saint-Simon, in spite of his seniority, declared that he was willing to

serve under Lafayette's orders. Life seemed beautiful!

Beautiful, but difficult. Washington and Rochambeau, even though they were on the road, still had a great distance to travel before reaching Virginia. Meanwhile, young Lafayette had to supervise everything — find food for the French forces in a country that had already been pillaged. Naturally, De Grasse was impatient to attack. Lafayette tried to persuade him to wait until Washington arrived. This showed how much Lafayette had matured. If he had yielded to

De Grasse's wishes, he could have claimed much of the victory for himself, but such a victory would have cost a great many lives, while a regular siege would achieve the same result with few casualties. But above everything, he wanted Washington to share in the glory of the victory. He sent an urgent message to Rochambeau: "Come quickly, my general."

Finally, the allied armies arrived. For the first time in the entire campaign, the naval forces and the land forces were able to work together effectively. If the land forces had not arrived on schedule, De Grasse probably would have carried out his threat to return to the West Indies. Even as it was, all the authority of Rochambeau and all the diplomacy of Lafayette were needed to persuade him to stay. The siege began immediately. The French and Americans competed enthusiastically to see which army could construct the better trenches and destroy more of the enemy's fortifications.

Always hopeful that Clinton might arrive and relieve him, Cornwallis had dug in at Yorktown.

On October 10, the allied bombardment began, and Washington himself fired the first shot. The enemy had built two redoubts from which they could cannonade the allied lines. The redoubts had to be taken by assault. The allies decided to share the job. The Marquis was to attack one of them with his American light infantry; the Baron de Vioménil, the other, with his Auvergne Grenadiers.

Rochambeau had previously commanded this regiment. Before the attack, he went into the trenches and spoke to the soldiers: "Boys, if I need you tonight, I hope you won't forget that we have served together in that fine regiment, *Auvergne sans tache* [Spotless Auvergne], a name that it deserves and has lived up to ever since it was formed."

The Auvergne Grenadiers showed themselves to be quite as brave as ever. As for Lafayette's Americans, they captured the redoubt assigned to them at bayonet point in ten minutes. This time the Marquis could not resist the temptation to make a gallant gesture, and he sent word to

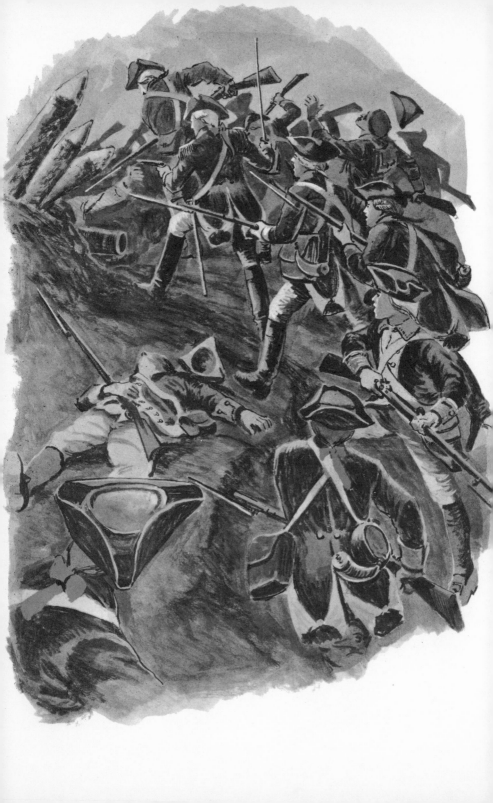

the Baron de Vioménil that if the Auvergne Grenadiers needed help, the American troops could
lend a hand, having already completed their
mission.

The capture of the redoubts soon brought an
end to the siege. The allied generals were surprised that Cornwallis had not resisted longer.
Evidently he realized that further fighting was
futile, for on October 17, 1781, he decided to
capitulate.

"I thought," he declared, "that it would have
been wicked and inhuman to sacrifice this small
band of gallant soldiers."

The surrender was signed on the morning of
the 19th. The English troops were ordered to
march between the two conquering armies — the
Americans on one side, the French on the other.
The victors maintained a respectful silence. In
order not to humiliate the defeated soldiers,
Washington and Rochambeau allowed no civil-
ians to attend the ceremony. Washington would
have permitted the English to keep their colors,
but Lafayette reminded him that when the

American general Lincoln had been defeated, the English had not granted him the honors of war.

Cornwallis was not present; he had made it known that he was ill. General O'Hara, who replaced him, wished to surrender his sword to Rochambeau. Rochambeau declined and indicated Washington. And Washington, declining also, designated General Lincoln, who took the sword and then immediately returned it. On the following day Lafayette asked to meet Cornwallis, against whom he had fought for so long. The English commander told him, "I am aware of the humanity of the French toward prisoners and I commend my poor army to you."

Evidently he wished to curry favor with the French, but he had forgotten that Lafayette was also an American general. His compliments were coldly received.

"You know, my lord, that the Americans as well have always been humane toward captured enemies," replied the Marquis.

Lafayette wrote home: "The play is over; the curtain has just gone down on the fifth act."

LAFAYETTE'S LETTER to Maurepas announcing "the end of the fifth act" and the happy ending of the play arrived in France only a few days before the Marquis himself. Lauzun, who delivered the letter, found Maurepas on his deathbed, but the good news made the old man smile with pleasure—for the last time. Seven days later, Lafayette landed in France and immediately took the first mail coach for Paris.

On the day of his arrival, Paris was celebrating the recent birth of the new crown prince—the Dauphin. The Queen herself was to attend the reception at the City Hall. Soldiers had to hold back the enormous crowds which filled the streets.

Lafayette went directly home to the Noailles mansion on the rue St.-Honoré. When he passed by, the crowd recognized him because of his American uniform and began to shout *"Vive Lafayette!"*

To his disappointment, Adrienne was not at home. The whole family, including his wife, had gone to the City Hall for the ceremony. But crowds are like a living telegraph system. Soon the Queen learned that the Marquis had returned. Although the reception was still in progress, she

graciously placed one of her own carriages at Adrienne's disposal to take her home to join her husband. When the people saw the royal coach driving up the rue St.-Honoré, they began shouting their approval. Lafayette emerged from the house just in time to gather his young wife into his arms, for, on seeing him, she had fainted with joy.

The first days that Lafayette spent in Paris were days of triumph. The King received him and made him a field marshal — a *maréchal* at

the age of twenty-four! His Sovereign then conferred upon him the coveted Cross of Saint Louis. He was popular with everyone — with the old courtiers because he was a good soldier and had given the English a beating, and with young people because he represented the popular new ideas of liberty and equality.

People cheered whenever he appeared — at the theater or the opera. At the opera one evening they were giving *Iphigenia in Aulis*. As the chorus began to sing *"Achille est couronné des mains de la Victoire"* (Achilles is crowned by the hands of Victory), the star, Mademoiselle Torlay, went to Lafayette's box with a wreath of laurel in her hand, and the entire house went wild.

He was also popular with the common people. One day the market women — the fishwives, the vegetable women — closed up their stands and, dressed in their best, went in a body to the Noailles mansion to present branches of laurel.

But all this popularity did not go to his head. In spite of his youth, he had already become a man who was more interested in the welfare of his country than in his own personal glory. Ministers came to him for advice. Vergennes, the Foreign Minister, had a high opinion of his judgment. Now that the war against England was won, it was necessary to win the peace, and this problem concerned not only the United States, but France and Spain as well. A strong country like England could certainly have continued fighting if she had felt it was to her advantage, but public opinion was against the war. The wealthy merchants wanted once again to do business with England and hoped for a reconciliation.

The Americans had sent John Adams to Paris to conduct peace negotiations. It was not a good choice. Although he was an honest and cultured man, Adams seemed to feel that anyone who did not agree with him was wrong. Franklin's popularity in Paris both amazed and irritated Adams. Franklin loved the French, but Adams, who did not speak a word of their language, couldn't stand them. Lafayette tried to smooth things over. He told John Adams that the most elementary good manners indicated that he should call on Vergennes, which so far he had failed to do.

All these slow, painful diplomatic negotiations irritated Lafayette. He was glad to be called to Madrid to assist the American diplomatic representative there. While he was in Spain, he learned that the peace treaty had been signed. Admiral d'Estaing proposed to the King of Spain, Charles III, that he should name Lafayette as governor of Jamaica.

"Certainly not!" replied the King. "He'd try to make a republic out of it."

And he probably was not far wrong!

Lafayette returned to Paris for the baptism of his newborn daughter. He decided to name her Virginia in remembrance of the state where he had won his great victory. Franklin laughingly said to him, "I hope you'll have twelve more children so that you can name them in honor of the twelve other states!"

The Americans also were showering honors on Lafayette. The former officers of the American army had founded an association called the

Society of the Cincinnatus. They invited him to become a member and asked him to name other French officers on whom this distinction should be conferred. He recommended Rochambeau, Noailles, Lauzun, Du Portail, and a number of others. Those who were forgotten complained bitterly. Lafayette was obliged to draw up a supplementary list and even to include Conway, who had plotted with Gates against Washington, and whom he thoroughly disliked. Peace, as well as war, has its problems — less acute, perhaps, but thorny nevertheless.

Naturally, he wanted to return in triumph to his home town of Chavaniac, the Auvergne village where he was born — to visit again that gloomy castle where he had passed his boyhood in the company of an abbé and three old ladies. The peasants of the village were there awaiting him, assembled on the broad terrace with its mountain view. First they cheered him — then, they began to complain. The harvest had been poor; they didn't have enough wheat. However, the overseer of the estate had already boasted to the Marquis that he had been able to lay in a reserve supply of grain.

"This is the time," he told Lafayette, "to sell it at a fat profit."

"This is rather the time," Lafayette replied, "to give it away."

He told everyone he met that he hoped there would be a big change in France. In his drawing room he hung a framed copy of the American Declaration of Independence. Beside it there was an empty frame.

"That's where we're going to put the French Declaration of Independence!" he declared.

He decided that he should have a home of his own in Paris and bought one at No. 81 rue de Bourbon. While it was being furnished, Adrienne visited Chavaniac with him for the first time. While there, they received word from Washington; his modest and gracious letter told them that he had retired from public life and had settled down at Mount Vernon.

"At length, my dear Marquis, I am become a

private citizen on the banks of the Potomac; and under the shadow of my own vine and my own fig tree, far from the bustle of a camp and the busy scene of public life, I am solacing myself with . . . tranquil enjoyments . . . Envious of none, I am determined to be pleased with all; and this, my dear friend, being the order for my march, I will move gently down the stream of life until I sleep with my fathers."

Although Lafayette was still too young to subscribe fully to such a philosophy, he could, nevertheless, admire it. He felt a very strong urge to see his "commander-in-chief and his spiritual father" once again. He replied that in the near future Washington could expect him to arrive at Mount Vernon to take a cup of tea. So when Adrienne left Paris to spend the summer at Chavaniac with the three children, Lafayette set sail on July 1, 1784, for New York, a city he had never seen. During his former visits to the United States it had been in the hands of the English.

He was greeted as New York still greets its

distinguished guests — with flowers, flags, shouting crowds, a triumphal ride through the town in an open carriage. His former officers gave a banquet for him.

From New York, he went to Philadelphia where he received the same enthusiastic welcome. Lafayette was delighted. He loved to be popular, to be acclaimed by the crowd. He was very touched when a city in Pennsylvania was named after him. But he was especially eager to see his friend Washington once more.

Soon he was on his way to Mount Vernon. There he spent eleven happy days with Washington, riding with him over the fields of the great plantation. Lafayette would never forget Martha Washington's baked Virginia ham and her homemade peach brandy. Naturally, the two men talked about the war. Now that it was over, even the desperate days at Valley Forge seemed wonderful. They also discussed politics. Lafayette had ambitious plans for France. Washington advised him to progress slowly. The Marquis would gladly have stayed longer, but he had so little time! He must tear himself away from the pleasures of Mount Vernon.

The Commissioners of Congress, who were on their way to sign a treaty with the Mohawks and other tribes of the area, invited Lafayette to accompany them to Fort Schuyler in upstate New York. They remembered that in the past these savage warriors had adopted Lafayette and had given him the name of Kayewla. Lafayette was happy to accept; he liked the picturesque

Indian ceremonies. Nothing pleased him more than to sit on the ground by the campfire, smoking the peace pipe with the proud, gaudily painted native chiefs. Lafayette, who had become a real diplomat, knew how to talk to them; he told them of the King of France, who was their friend. He advised them to remain on good terms with the United States.

"Grasshopper," who was the official orator of the Six Nations, presented him with a string of beads which Montcalm had once given the Indians as a token of peace. Lafayette-Kayewla, after an eloquent speech, returned the beads to his hosts as a symbol of his friendship, and the Six Nations signed a treaty of peace with the young republic. It was another success to Lafayette's credit.

The time had now come for him to embark on the French frigate *Nymph*. Before returning home, however, he decided to visit Virginia once again. Washington accompanied him to Richmond. Both Virginia and Maryland conferred honorary citizenship on Lafayette and on all his male descendants.

Washington and Lafayette had decided to part at Annapolis. From there, Lafayette would proceed to New York to board his ship. Their farewell was simple, for Washington had a horror of emotional scenes. Both men, however, were deeply touched. Lafayette was sad to take leave of the man who had helped mold his character and to whom he felt he owed everything. For Washington, this separation was the more melancholy, when he remembered that this might be the last time that he would ever see his "foster son." Lafayette insisted that he would come back to America every year, but Washington only smiled, shook his head, got into his carriage, and drove off.

A few days later Lafayette reached New York. He boarded the *Nymph* to the thunder of a cannon salute. A letter from Washington was waiting for him: "I often asked myself, as our carriages separated, whether that was the last

sight I ever should have of you? And though I wished to say No, my fear answered Yes."

Lafayette, before setting sail, immediately replied that he was horrified by such an idea and that he would often return to America to visit the dearest friend he had on earth.

As he well knew deep in his heart, however, it would be difficult to keep his promise, for he would be increasingly absorbed by new responsibilities and by the task of making a new and more democratic France. He realized that it would be a long time before he would again cross the Atlantic. The days of his youth had passed.

WASHINGTON WAS right. The two men were never to see each other again. Lafayette, on his return to France, was caught up in the French Revolution and the events which followed and was unable to return to America. Of course, he corresponded with his friends. American diplomatic representatives in Europe often asked his advice, and he worked to maintain good relations between the two countries. The people of Nantucket sent him "the biggest cheese in the world," made from a day's production of milk collected from every farm on the island. The State of Virginia presented to the city of Paris a portrait bust of Lafayette by the great sculptor Houdon!

Thus the United States continued to honor him, but Lafayette realized that he must remain in France.

Why? Because he sensed that something important was in the air, and he wanted to be the "Washington of France." He and his friends who had fought in America called for the convocation of the national assembly known as the "Estates-General," in order to pave the way for certain necessary reforms. It seemed improbable, but such an assembly *was* called, in 1789, and Lafayette was a leading member.

The Court, and certain conservative aristocrats, mistrusted him, but the people adored him. He was thirty-two years old. In Paris, crowds cheered when he appeared in the street. He was named commanding general of the National Guard by popular acclamation. He hoped that needed reforms in France could be achieved through a peaceful revolution in an atmosphere of order and harmony and with the consent of the King, who would become a kind of president of his country. Men are not so easy to lead, however. Nothing happened as Lafayette wished. The people committed blind acts of violence, and the King, frightened by their excesses, tried to take flight.

Lafayette, somewhat too concerned with maintaining his own popularity, failed to act with the firmness that was necessary. It soon became apparent that the Court detested him because he was too friendly with the people, and the people disliked him because he defended the King. In the National Assembly, violent extremists like Robespierre and Danton attacked him. When he took command of the Army of the North in order to defend his country against invasion, there were those who went so far as to claim that "liberty is in danger so long as Lafayette has an army."

When the monarchy fell and Louis XVI was seized, Lafayette was forced to resign his command. He was immediately arrested by the enemy — the Prussians and the Austrians. They imprisoned him in the fortress of Olmütz, where he received the harshest treatment. He appealed to Washington for help. But as President of the

United States, the General could not very well intervene directly in European affairs and thus provide European powers with a pretext for intervening in America. As a private citizen, however, he aided Lafayette by sending him money, and he invited his godson George to be his guest in the United States. But he could not free Lafayette from prison. Lafayette's wife, the devoted and courageous Adrienne — all of whose immediate relatives had been guillotined — went voluntarily to join him at Olmütz and shared his suffering.

When Napoleon came to power, the Marquis was finally liberated. Soon, however, he quarreled with the new master of France. Lafayette had dreamed of a republic on the American model—but obviously Napoleon was no Washington. When Lafayette saw that Napoleon was making himself an emperor, he decided to retire to the country property which his wife had inherited—the Château de la Grange, near Paris. Here he remained for twelve years, steadfastly refusing to have anything to do with Napoleon Bonaparte, the Master of Europe. "Everyone has fallen into line," said the Emperor, "except Lafayette . . . He's all ready to start trouble again."

In 1807 the faithful Adrienne died, and Lafayette was deeply stricken. He refused, however, to leave La Grange. Many Americans came to see him there. When the Napoleonic Empire fell, when France was invaded once again, when King Louis XVIII was restored to power, Lafayette conducted himself with a patriotism that was liberal and moderate, without a trace of fanaticism. But the old aristocrats, who had now come back into power, hated him because he had always been a champion of democracy.

Once again he went into retirement at La Grange. However, he felt a strong desire to see America once more. It was now the year 1824. Nearly half a century had rolled by since the signing of the Declaration of Independence. The struggling Republic that he had aided in its fight for liberty had now become a great and powerful nation.

When President Monroe invited him to return as the guest of the American people, he accepted with pleasure. New York City gave him the rousing welcome he deserved. Everywhere flags flew which bore the legend "Welcome, Lafayette"; everywhere there were cheering crowds. Lafayette was now sixty-seven years old. It was very moving to realize that this elegant old gentleman was "the Boy" who had been one of America's staunchest friends in her time of greatest need. Hundreds of towns sent him invitations, and he made a triumphal cross-country tour.

He was impressed, wherever he went, by the

enormous progress of the young Republic. Prosperous cities had arisen on sites that he had known as marshes or desolate brushlands. He returned to Philadelphia where one summer day he had been received by the Congress as a mere adventurer. On the present occasion the great city welcomed him as an honored guest. From here, he proceeded on a pilgrimage to Mount Vernon. Washington, his foster father, his friend, his revered commander-in-chief, was dead. Lafayette tarried long beside the tomb, his eyes filled with tears.

He also visited Yorktown. Instead of his motley band of soldiers, ill-fed and ill-clothed, here was a well-disciplined, well-equipped army smartly passing in review. He well remembered that day so long ago when the French troops, transported by De Grasse, were scheduled to land — a day on which he told his men: "Wash your uniforms and wash yourselves as well, so that we'll make a good impression." Those had been desperate times, but as Lafayette looked back on them, they seemed very happy times, too, for then he was young, and hardship mattered little.

President Monroe organized an impressive banquet for him on New Year's Day of 1825. At its conclusion, the President arose and proposed a toast to the Marquis, "the great apostle of liberty." Lafayette, in reply, expressed the hope that the friendship between France and the United States might last forever. "One day," he declared, "our two countries will be called upon to save the world."

He had no desire to hurry home to France. He loved popularity and for many years, for very honorable reasons, he had been deprived of it. It was wonderful to bask once again in the warmth of affection and of universal acclaim. He visited the little New York town of Fayetteville which had been named in his honor. Then he went on to Boston where he presided at a banquet which took place on Bunker Hill. There he proposed a toast—"to sacred resistance to oppression."

Did he still hope that he might one day become the champion of such a cause in his own country? It is quite possible. Lafayette was a man who never gave up hope, either for humanity, or for his country, or for himself. And the final period of his life would show that he had reason to hope.

But if he was to be useful to the world, he must return to France, where his own reputation had been enhanced by the enthusiastic reception he had received in America. For the trip home, the American Congress had put a frigate at his disposal, as they had during the Revolution. It was named the *Brandywine* in commemoration of the river on whose shores Lafayette had first seen action, and where he had first been wounded.

On the eve of his departure, the city of New York honored him with a magnificent ball. It was held at Castle Garden, near the old Battery, and was a great success. The French guests were surprised by the elegance and the luxury which they saw about them. They asked themselves if it were all a dream — this fairyland that had been created out of the wilderness that Columbus had discovered. When Lafayette entered the ball-room, lines of distinguished guests were present to shake his hand. He circulated among them, affable yet dignified, "as gracious as a king." The elderly Marquis was like a father, come home again to his family after a long separation.

The newly elected President, John Quincy Adams, was present. He proposed a toast to the birthdays of Washington and Lafayette. Lafayette replied with a toast to "the Fourth of July, the birthday of Liberty in two hemispheres."

Finally, on September 6, 1825, he boarded the *Brandywine*. The trip had re-inspired him. He had relived in memory the most significant period of his life, and this experience had filled him with renewed faith and self-confidence. In America he could witness the benefits of liberty. The prodigious success of the United States had restored his faith in liberty and democracy, a faith that had been somewhat shaken by the terrors of the French Revolution and the tyranny of the Empire.

In France once again he saw that the people were as moved as he had been by the welcome which faraway America had given a brave Frenchman. Once more he was cheered as he stepped ashore. Adrienne was no longer there,

however, to welcome him to La Grange or to the handsome Noailles mansion. No longer did the haughty but still lovely Queen preside over the gay parties at Versailles. But the public still acclaimed him, those unknown friends who were very numerous indeed. When he arrived at La Grange, some distance from Paris, he found that a crowd of 4000 people had prepared a festive display of fireworks in his honor.

Many of the old and faithful comrades of his adventurous youth had never forgotten his courageous deeds and all the sacrifices he had made for the cause of liberty. For them, he still represented a force on which France might need to call one day. Five years later, in July, 1830, the French people arose again in revolt against a regime disrespectful of its rights. Despite his age, Lafayette left retirement to be instrumental in the choice of a new constitutional monarch willing to accept the tricolor flag of Republican France, a king who promised to respect the Declaration of Human Rights.

When Lafayette died in 1834 and the news

reached the American Congress, all members stood in silence to pay homage to the young General who had remained throughout his long life a staunch friend of the United States. Congress went into mourning, and the Capitol was draped in black. Both French and American flags flew at half-mast. John Quincy Adams, the ex-President, appeared personally before Congress to pay his respects to the man who had done so much to help the American nation win its independence.

The United States has never forgotten its debt of gratitude to Lafayette. In 1918, when the first American troops arrived to fight beside the French in World War I, General Pershing declared, "Lafayette, we are here."

Men die, but their heroic deeds leave a shining wake in the waters of time.

*Those who enjoyed this book and want
to learn more about the American Revolution would also be interested in other North
Stars dealing with the same period:*

*Young Washington's part in the French
and Indian War and the alliance between
the Iroquois and the British during the Revolution is described in:*

Index